In memory of a good friend and colleague,
Skip Helsing

Contents

The Nonprofit Lobbying Guide

Second Edition

by Bob Smucker

ISBN 0-929556-00-3

10   Special Issues and Regulations   65

Preface

This is a handbook for volunteers and staff of charitable organizations, especially new volunteers and staff, to help them take advantage of the liberal rules for lobbying by charities.* These rules make it possible for charities to lobby freely for their causes and clients. It is very clear that the federal government, including Congress and the Internal Revenue Service (IRS), supports lobbying by charities. Congress sent that unambiguous message when it enacted the generous provisions in the 1976 lobby law.** The same message came from the IRS, in new regulations issued on August 31, 1990, which support both the spirit and the intent of the 1976 legislation. Together, the law and the new regulations provide plenty of leeway for charities to lobby.

It is my hope that this book will encourage volunteers and staff of charities to be bold in their lobbying to enact laws and pass appropriations that will aid those they seek to serve. I intend the book especially for volunteers and staff who are concerned about helping to achieve greater equity in the sharing of this nation's vast resources—people who are working to change public policy in order to assist the most vulnerable in our society.

Those who are new to charity volunteer or staff work may be inclined to place lobbying at the bottom of the list of abilities they want to develop. They may believe that it is too complex to master, perhaps a bit tainted, and maybe even illegal, or they may assign it low priority because they already have a number of other well-honed skills that they can immediately put to work for their organizations. Once involved in the process, however, most people find that lobbying is not difficult to learn and that the organizing skills they already possess are easily transferred to influencing legislation for the people they serve. And, far from its being disreputable or illegal, most people discover that lobbying is a perfectly legitimate, reasonable, and personally rewarding way of fulfilling their organizations' public purposes.

* Charitable organization, as used throughout this book, refers only to organizations that are tax-exempt under Section 501(c)(3) of the Internal Revenue Code. Private foundations are tax exempt under that Section but (with important exceptions) are not permitted to lobby.

** The term *1976 lobby law* is used throughout this book for legislation passed in 1976—Section 1307 of PL 94-455—that clarifies and expands lobbying by tax-exempt charities under Section 501(c)(3) of the Internal Revenue Code. The legislation does not apply to churches, their integrated auxiliaries, or conventions or associations of churches that at their own request, remain under the pre-1976 provision. These groups may lobby, but remain under the "insubstantial" rule, explained on pp. 62–63.

In Part Three, six charity leaders tell their stories about how much lobbying has meant for their causes, their organizations, and their lives. Several also tell what they have learned about how to lobby effectively. In particular, David Cohen, co-founder of The Advocacy Institute and a man who has been involved in some of the country's most important public policy struggles of the past 35 years, offers many insights about public interest lobbying. David discusses how lobbying has changed, what these changes mean for public interest lobbyists, and what combination of values, skills, attitudes, and knowledge make someone an effective public interest lobbyist.

If you are just getting started, the lobbying tips offered in this book should be helpful as you make your first contacts with legislators. But even if you are not altogether new to lobbying and are looking for additional ideas for your work, you will find a full menu. If you are more experienced at lobbying but are, for example, at the crucial point where you seek a sponsor for legislation that your group wants introduced, I think you will find the strategic advice in this book helpful.

Organization of the Book

The Nonprofit Lobbying Guide is divided into three parts. Part One provides how-to information on lobbying by charities. Almost every national organization has written a manual on how to influence legislation. Each charity's organizational structure is different, and so it is not possible to provide detailed how-to information that will fit every group's needs. There are, however, some approaches to lobbying that seem to accomplish the job for almost all charities, and those approaches are included here.

Part Two gives information, in laypersons' language, concerning a number of technical questions: How much lobbying by charities is legal under federal law? How do the new IRS regulations on lobbying by charities affect the amount of lobbying you can do? Can a private foundation grant funds to a charity that lobbies? What information on the views of a candidate for public office can a charity provide to its members? What are the federal requirements for disclosure of lobbying activities?

Most of the technical information applies equally to lobbying at the federal, state, and local levels. Part One, the how-to section, however, deals principally with federal legislation, although much of the information is readily adapted to state or local lobbying.

Part Three includes statements from six noted charity leaders—ranging from long-time lobbyists to life-long volunteers—about why they lobby in the public interest. The main purpose of this section is to encourage staff of charities, especially those beginning their professional lives, to consider lobbying for charities as a career choice. The statements provide ample evidence of the enormous satisfaction that comes from charity lobbying by both volunteers and staff.

These six leaders collectively have decades of experience with charity lobbying, and many of them offer some very practical lessons in how to do it well. This is particularly true of the longer essay by David Cohen, co-founder of The Advocacy Institute, who has been involved in many of this country's most important lobbying campaigns during the past three decades.

INDEPENDENT SECTOR often receives questions from the Members about real-life situations regarding what constitutes lobbying or voter education activities. Resource A provides 10 examples of such questions along with answers.

In all candor, parts of this book may be less than compelling and will not tempt you to burn the midnight oil. Therefore, I have included a summary in Resource B for readers interested in skimming the book quickly for the main points.

The other resources contain material helpful to lobbyists. Resource C offers answers to some often-asked questions about lobbying; Resource D reprints the article "How to Win the Advocacy Game," by Doug Siglin; Resource E consists of examples of lobbying materials to help you get started; Resource F reprints IRS form 5768, which a charity must file to elect to come under the provisions of the 1976 lobby law; and Resource G lists addresses of organizations that are mentioned in the book so that you can contact them for additional information.

This book, especially Part Two, is intended to provide enough information so that new volunteers and staff will have an elementary understanding of lobbying and will know where to find more information. It is not intended to replace legal counsel. If you have questions regarding the technical information, you should seek legal advice. However, it is important to keep in mind that lawyers, with some notable exceptions, tend to be much too cautious in counseling charities about lobbying. Their usual advice is to tread very lightly, if at all, in the lobbying arena. That's questionable advice, at best, stemming from the fact that too many lawyers are not well acquainted with the lobbying law. It is perfectly acceptable to probe the advice of lawyers, so that you can be very certain that they know the latitude permitted to charities under the law, including the 1976 lobby law.

The Nonprofit Lobbying Guide grew out of what I have learned over more than 25 years from lobbying on behalf of charitable organizations and working with some extraordinarily talented volunteer and staff lobbyists. I hope it will be a useful guide, but it is simply that: a guide. You don't need to know or practice most of what is in this book to get started lobbying. Don't be put off by what may appear to be a mountain of information. Skim through it, take what you need—and good luck!

Acknowledgments

Virtually all the information in Chapter Nine was drawn from materials prepared for INDEPENDENT SECTOR by Walter B. Slocombe of Caplin & Drysdale, Washington, D.C. I am grateful that INDEPENDENT SECTOR and Mr. Slocombe have permitted me to use that important information.

Substantial portions of Chapter Ten were taken, with permission, from writings of Sandford F. Brandt. As a volunteer for both the National Mental Health Association and INDEPENDENT SECTOR, Brandt has written on many issues related to lobbying. I am grateful that he permitted me to excerpt so fully from his writings. I am also grateful for his very helpful suggestions on this book. Information in Chapter Ten on Gifts to Federal Lawmakers and on the Lobby Disclosure Act of 1995, were taken from writings by Eric Wentworth, for INDEPENDENT SECTOR.

I am also grateful for the help from Gary Bass and Patrick Lemmon for the assistance in Chapters Three and Five where I give information on the new technologies important to lobbying communications by charities. Gary Bass wrote much of the Section on OMB Circular A-122.

Final decisions regarding the content of this book were mine, but I owe much to others for their critiques and suggestions. They include Mathew Ahmann, Gary Bass, the late Philip Bernstein, Gregory L. Colvin, John Colvin, the late Lee Goodman, Julee Kryder-Coe, Brian O'Connell, Hilda Robbins, Walter B. Slocombe, Barbara Mills Smucker, Thomas A. Troyer, and Edward T. Weaver. I am especially indebted to Brenda Lee and Jill Yothers, who typed and edited numerous revisions of the manuscript.

Bob Smucker
Washington, D.C.
January 1999

The Author

Bob Smucker, vice president for government relations at INDEPENDENT SECTOR from 1980 to 1998, has worked with nonprofit organizations since 1957. His background includes more than 25 years as a lobbyist at the local, state, and national levels.

From 1957 to 1971, he worked in Pennsylvania with local mental health associations, as well as with the Pennsylvania Mental Health Association, a statewide citizens' advocacy organization. During that time, his lobbying activities included a leading role in the enactment of legislation, passed in 1966, that provided for the development and funding of community mental health centers. He was also involved in a successful effort to get the United Steel Workers of America to include ambulatory mental health coverage in its nationwide contract with the steel industry.

From 1971 to 1979, Smucker was director of public policy for the National Mental Health Association. During that time, he was centrally involved in the enactment of the 1976 lobby law, which clarified and expanded the lobbying rights of nonprofits. He was also a principal actor in obtaining continued federal funding for community mental health centers. He had chief responsibility for developing a mental health coalition that brought successful litigation resulting in the release of $127 million in impounded mental health research and training funds by the Department of Health, Education and Welfare. He also provided staff leadership for litigation brought by the National Mental Health Association and other groups in the successful effort to end unpaid patient labor in state mental hospitals.

The author's activities with INDEPENDENT SECTOR have included working with the advocacy community to organize and provide leadership for the coalition that convinced the Internal Revenue Service (IRS) to withdraw restrictive proposed regulations governing lobbying. That coalition also worked with the IRS to develop sound new regulations. The author also had senior staff responsibility in developing and providing coordination for a coalition that acted to have the Office of Management and Budget withdraw proposed regulations that would have greatly curtailed the rights of nonprofits to lobby with the funds they receive from private contributions. In 1995-96, he had a lead role, again working with the advocacy community in turning aside a number of efforts by Congressman Ernest Istook (R-OK) to sharply reduce or disallow lobbying by nonprofits that receive federal funds. Smucker has also had principal staff responsibility for INDEPENDENT SECTOR's involvement in three Supreme Court cases related to the fund-raising activities of nonprofits. All three cases were decided in favor of the First Amendment rights of nonprofits.

Smucker currently is project director of Charity Lobbying in the Public Interest, a project of INDEPENDENT SECTOR, an initiative whose objective is to encourage nonprofits to consider lobbying as an important, effective means of achieving their missions.

Part One

How to
Lobby

1

Anyone Can Lobby

The personnel manager of a large midwestern manufacturing company once told me that job descriptions, even for junior executives, are often drawn up by well-intentioned but unknowing staff to include requirements so demanding that not even the president of the company could fulfill them. How-to books can suffer from the same problem. They don't distinguish between what you have to know and all the other things that could be helpful but are not absolutely essential.

The information in this book is not a description of what you need to know—or the experience you must have—to get started. Nobody, not even the most seasoned lobbyist, does all or even close to half of it. All your organization needs as you start lobbying is a staff person or volunteer who has a little knowledge of lobbying techniques; has an elementary understanding of how the legislative process works in whatever body you are planning to lobby, whether Congress, the state legislature, county government, or the city council; can organize a government relations committee that will consider the legislative issues your organization may want to tackle; can organize volunteers to form a legislative network; and has a passing knowledge of the law governing lobbying by nonprofits.

Much of the information you need to start lobbying probably is readily available in your own community. A number of nonprofits, civic organizations, and public-spirited citizens have been

lobbying for years and would be complimented if your group asked them for help in understanding the areas just described. For example, the League of Women Voters could be particularly helpful. Several other groups, including environmental organizations and most of the major health organizations (such as the heart, lung, cancer, and disability groups), would have considerable lobbying knowledge and would probably have affiliates in your community. Also, INDEPENDENT SECTOR and Charity Lobbying in the Public Interest can provide advice to help you get started.

Lobbying Law

Before you start lobbying, you should know a little about the law governing lobbying by nonprofits. The 1976 lobby law and regulations provide very generous lobbying limits. You should know what the law says about how much of your organization's annual expenditures can go for lobbying and what activities are defined as lobbying, but the most important point to keep in mind is that the law permits ample room for all the lobbying your group will probably want to undertake. It is very simple to elect to come under the provisions of the law (see Chapter 9 for details).

If you have questions about whether the amount of lobbying you want to conduct is within the law, discuss it with other nonprofits that lobby extensively, as well as with your attorney. But remember that attorneys almost always err on the side of extreme caution in counseling nonprofits about lobbying. If you ask your lawyer for advice, be certain that he or she not only knows the lobby law well (only a few do) but, even more important, also is familiar with the experience of organizations that have lobbied under the law. Groups have found plenty of legal latitude for lobbying, without jeopardizing their tax-exempt status.

The Legislative Process and Your Lobbyist

It is important to have a volunteer or staff person in your organization who knows the basics of how your legislature works, because you will need that information to know how to target your efforts. For example, you may be trying to block legislation averse to your group, help support pending legislation backed by your organization, or arrange the introduction of legislation vital to your group. In the typical legislature, to achieve any of these aims, you will have to gain the support of the committee designated to consider your issue. It follows that you will need to know something about the composition of that committee. For example, if you are seeking to have legislation introduced, it is usually possible to recruit a committee member to introduce your bill. But you won't want just any member. You will want a person of influence, and that usually means a senior committee member whose party is in the majority and therefore controls the committee.

It is incidentally helpful to know that many decisions on legislation are often made in a last-minute frenzy as legislators prepare to adjourn for the legislative session. The lobbyist (whether a volunteer or a paid staff member) who is following your issue in the legislature should have enough understanding of how the

legislative process works so that your group can make the right move at the right place and time (for example, knowing whether to support or oppose an amendment that suddenly comes up). Your lobbyist needs to recognize, for example, whether this is the last chance to modify your bill or if you still have a reasonable chance for the changes you want in the other house of the legislature. A lobbyist who knows (among other things) the best legislator to introduce your bill and how and when decisions are made in your legislature is referred to as an *inside lobbyist.*

Having a seasoned insider available to your organization can save you enormous time and effort. Perhaps volunteers or staff people bring such experience to your group from their work with other nonprofits. If not, such groups as the League of Women Voters can help your group develop an understanding of how your legislature really works. Former legislators or those currently in office can also be very helpful. Nationally, the Advocacy Institute, INDEPENDENT SECTOR, and Charity Lobbying in the Public Interest, among other organizations, can provide how-to information about lobbying by nonprofits (see Resource G).

If you have the funds, it is possible to hire a good, experienced lobbying consultant. If you choose that route, check with other nonprofits whose opinions you value highly and who have used consultants to lobby. The best way of being certain that you are getting the right person is to check his or her track record with other groups. Consultants should be pleased to give you the names of groups for which they have lobbied.

The Government Relations Committee and the Legislative Network

Your organization will need to set up a government relations committee to consider how your group's program can be furthered by legislative initiatives. The committee will also establish legislative priorities and provide direction for the group's lobbying efforts. A strong government relations committee that represents a broad cross-section of your community can add immeasurably to the impact of your lobbying efforts. In using a government relations committee, it is enormously important to hold firmly to one top legislative priority, rather than following the more common route of trying to work on many issues at once. (This point and others are covered in Chapter 7.)

A nonprofit's principal lobbying power resides in the number of its members that it can get behind its legislation. To achieve that objective, most groups set up a legislative network to mobilize the grassroots network (see Chapter 4). At the minimum, your network should assign *one* volunteer, capable of enlisting others in his or her community, as a contact person for *each* member of the legislative committee(s) that will act on your bill. If there are 20 members of a legislative committee that

will act on your bill, 20 contact persons should be recruited.

Establishing and maintaining the network takes time and commitment because it is tedious, time-consuming work. It is easy to put off establishing a network and even easier to neglect it once it is set up. A nonprofit neglects its network at great risk, however. Without a network, there may be no chance to mobilize broad support on short notice. That kind of quick mobilization may be needed repeatedly during a legislative campaign.

In short, you need very little to get started. As we have seen, it helps to have a volunteer or a staff person who has an elementary understanding of basic lobbying techniques and of the lobbying process, as well as some organizing skills. As in all activities that involve people, common sense helps immeasurably.

Don't be put off by the amount of information in this book. If you can pick up a pen or the phone, you can lobby. Just go ahead. Get started, and keep in mind that lobbying and the legislative process are not nearly as complicated or difficult as lobbyists would have you believe.

2

The Nonprofit Lobbyist and the Legislative Process

A nonprofit's power to affect legislation comes from its grassroots strength—the quality and number of letters, other communications, and personal contacts its members make with legislators. Every one of an organization's members who communicates with a legislator is, in a very real sense, a lobbyist. Nevertheless, every organization that participates in the legislative process needs a volunteer or staff lobbyist who has some in-depth knowledge of the legislative process and can help provide direction for the group's legislative activities. This chapter describes the work of that principal lobbyist. A nonprofit's principal power does not reside in its lobbyist at the capital, because he or she does not live, work, and vote in the legislator's district. But a skilled lobbyist, whether a volunteer or a paid staff member, can contribute greatly to the development of the group's impact on legislation by providing effective liaison between the legislature and the nonprofit's grassroots.

Many nonprofits that are just starting to lobby recruit volunteers who have knowledge of and some experience with the legislative process. Over time, such groups often hire part-time or full-time staff or consultants to augment their lobbying capability. Many others continue very effectively with volunteers in the principal lobbying role. The important point is that you don't need a paid lobbyist to get started or even to conduct a sophisticated lobbying program. The League of Women Voters, for example, has few paid lobbyists, but the group is well known and respected for the skills its volunteers bring to government relations, including lobbying.

To get started, your lobbyist needs to know or be able to learn quickly the following things:

- The basics about the legislative process and the key committee members or other legislators who have either jurisdiction or influence over your legislation and can affect its movement;
- The details of the bill you are supporting and why its provisions are important to the legislators' constituents and to your organization; and
- The organizational structure of your group and how it communicates with its grassroots.

More important, the person who will be your lobbyist should have strong skills in interpersonal relations. A prospective lobbyist for your group may bring great understanding of government, its processes, and its key members, but if the relationship skills are absent, don't give him or her the job. This candidate will lack the most fundamental attribute of a good nonprofit lobbyist. It would be better to take on a person who has no lobbying experience but has demonstrated interpersonal skills and the ability to organize. Most such persons can be taught to lobby, but chances are that you will not be able to change the performance of the person who brings understanding of the process but lacks sound interpersonal skills.

You will be tempted to take the person who lacks the relationship skills but has the knowledge, especially if he or she is articulate. If you do, however, over time you will probably find yourself following after the lobbyist at the state capitol and trying to mend relationships. Worse yet, word won't get back to you about your lobbyist because of people's natural reluctance to pass along negative information; you will just find that your lobbyist is having difficulty gaining access. Again, if you have to make the choice, go with the relationship and organizing skills.

The principal responsibility of your organization's lobbyist is to work effectively for enactment of your group's legislation. The success or failure of your legislation depends considerably on how well your lobbyist can orchestrate the movement of your bill through the legislature and on how effective he or she is in mobilizing your grassroots. Both tasks require an understanding of the legislative process. More important, the movement of your legislation requires that you recruit a strong member of the legislature to take the lead on your measure.

The Legislative Process

You are interested in the legislative process because of something you want—or do not want—legislators to do. To be most effective in influencing the legislative process, you must have a feel for how it works.

Legislation begins with the executive (the president, the governor, and so on), or it starts with an individual member of the legislature. Once started, the legislation goes to committees of both houses, and then it is acted on by one house, after which it goes to the other house and finally to a conference committee. The conference committee, composed of members of both houses, works out any differences between versions of the legislation passed by the two houses. The measure ultimately goes to the executive, to be either signed into law or vetoed. At each step, the measure can be stopped, changed, or passed along to the next stage of the process. Those decisions are made by individual members of the committee to which the legislation is referred, or they are made by the full House or Senate if the measure has moved out of committee. Each step can be influenced by your organization, as can the executive's decision to sign or veto the bill.

The Nonprofit's Legislative Proposal

Legislation initiated by a nonprofit organization usually starts with a program idea that the group thinks would not only make good public policy but also help achieve its own mission. Typically, such a proposal is considered first by the nonprofit's government relations committee and then by its board. Next, according to the importance of the proposed legislative initiative, the proposal may go before the group's total membership. Early in this process, it will be important for the organization to get information about the viability of the legislative proposal from a person who knows both the legislature and the major forces that will be working for or against the measure.

Selecting Your Leader in the Legislature

The key step in the legislative process is moving your bill to a successful vote in committee. Virtually no major legislation is enacted without having been considered by committee. Once that hurdle is passed, prospects are usually good for the bill's enactment by that house. Central to your success is the strength of the committee member who has agreed to take the lead on your measure.

A skilled lobbyist, whether a volunteer or a staff member, can be enormously helpful to you in recruiting the right person. You will want to choose the most influential committee member of the party that controls the committee. Likewise, for bipartisan balance, you will also want to approach the strongest person from the minority side of the committee to join in leading the effort. Often, of course, you won't be able to enlist the most influential committee members; they will be very much in demand among many other groups. You may have to adjust your sights and turn to another consideration: commitment to your issue, another important criterion in selecting your leader. Recruiting a committee member who is influential but does not strongly support your measure can easily lead to disappointment and probably defeat, especially if your bill is competing in committee with other bills that the legislator supports more strongly.

A criterion of almost equal importance is the skill and commitment of the legislative staff person whom your legislative leader assigns to your measure. A strong, skilled staff person who likes your issue can sometimes compensate for his or her boss's modest interest and

power within the committee. Conversely, lack of skill and interest on the part of this staff member can add significantly to the difficulty of moving your measure through, even if the legislator has influence with the committee and likes your issue. On balance, a skilled staff person working for a legislator who has more than a passing interest in your bill is a strong combination. Knowledge about the influence and power of the actors, both legislators and staff, is what your lobbyist must bring to your organization.

Introducing Legislation

To have legislation drafted, a member of Congress may consult with the legislative counsel of the House or Senate to frame the ideas in suitable legislative language and form. In Congress, the legislation is introduced on the floor of the House and the Senate, and it is assigned a bill number. Members who introduce legislation are called sponsors, and they often submit statements to the *Congressional Record* providing the rationale for their support. A *Congressional Record* statement may be an important resource for a nonprofit in generating support for a measure. Often, the member of Congress also issues a press release or similar statement about the legislation, which describes the measure's importance in language that is easy for a nonprofit to adapt for use with its members.

After the legislation is introduced, the Rules Committee in each house assigns it to the committee responsible for considering its type of legislation. The nonprofit should seek bipartisan support for its proposal by recruiting strong backing from Democrats and Republicans on the committees to which the legislation is assigned. (The nonprofit's members will also be most likely to give their own strong support if both parties are well represented.)

Soon afterward, the sponsors may send a letter, called a "Dear Colleague" letter, to every member of their house or to every member of their committee, explaining why they have introduced the measure and inviting members of their house to sign on as cosponsors. Because the number of members who cosponsor a bill gives an indication of support for the measure, nonprofits, working through local affiliates, often strive hard to recruit a large number of cosponsors. The number of cosponsors is not the true test of a bill's strength, however. Its strength is tested in the committee to which it is referred.

Role of the Committee

After the bill is assigned to a committee, the chair of the committee sends it to the appropriate subcommittee for consideration. Favorable action on the measure at the subcommittee and full committee levels is almost always a "make or break" situation for the measure. If it succeeds in getting out of subcommittee (especially with a strong majority of members voting in support), it *usually* gets favorable consideration in the full committee. Full committees do not like to second-guess the work of their subcommittees, and so they are often inclined to accept in its entirety, or only with modest modifications, the legislation coming out of their subcommittees.

It is crucial that each member of the subcommittee be contacted by a number of constituents who support the legislation. That is the most important action that a nonprofit can take. If you can't get favorable action in subcommittee, your proposal will have little chance of becoming law. The next most important step is to contact all members of the full committee and enlist their support. A bill may be lodged in committee for a year or longer, so there is usually ample time for a nonprofit to generate continuing grassroots contact with committee members.

Subcommittees and full committees often hold hearings on legislation, to get the views of a diverse group of individuals, organizations, and businesses supporting or opposing a measure. Nonprofits are wise to work closely with committees in setting up hearings and ensuring that there will be witnesses who favor their positions (see Chapter 4). Hearings can be very important in building support for your proposal. Nevertheless, they pale by comparison with the importance of being certain that each committee member is contacted by a number of key constituents who support the legislation.

After hearings, a subcommittee meets to do its final decision making (called a *mark-up)* on the bill and votes on it. By the time the mark-up stage arrives, most members of the committee will have decided whether they support the measure, and so nonprofits dare not wait until that point to make their contacts. That work has to be done in the preceding weeks, months, and even years.

Representatives of the nonprofit will want to be present when the legislation is marked up. (Congressional mark-ups are often closed, and so you'll have to wait in the hall outside the conference room. Be assured that you will have plenty of company.) The sponsor of the legislation may find that the only way your proposal can receive a favorable vote is through compromise. The legislator or the legislator's staff person must be able, on a moment's notice, to contact a spokesperson for the nonprofit and find out whether the compromise is acceptable. Before the mark-up, the person speaking for the nonprofit has to have been given authority to negotiate a compromise.

There are several other important reasons for being present at a mark-up. Some committee members may still be undecided, and getting a last-minute word with them can be important. (But, again, don't rely on last-minute contacts; seldom will they win the day.) Another reason for being there is that, by your presence, you are sending a message to legislators that your organization is very interested in the outcome and will be reporting the committee's action to the members' constituents.

Action on the House and Senate Floors

If your bill fails to make it out of the House committee, it will be virtually impossible to get it considered by the full House. Because the House Rules Committee rarely permits a vote unless a measure has received favorable committee action, the committee vote in the House usually seals the fate of your measure.

In the Senate, leadership may agree to allow a bill to be considered by the full Senate, even if the bill has lost in committee, especially if the committee vote was close. When the Senate sponsor of your legislation is successful in persuading leadership to bring your bill up for a vote in the full Senate, it may be

possible for you to win, if you have broad grassroots support. That can happen only if, in the months and even years before, you have been carefully building support for the measure among all members of the Senate.

The House/Senate Conference

After legislation has been passed by the House and the Senate, it goes to conference. Conferees are named by the chairs of the committees that have considered legislation. They are usually committee members with the most seniority or are chairs of particular subcommittees. Because conferees are often named a week or so before a conference, it is possible to get some last-minute messages in from the grassroots, if you are following the process closely. You will need to get the list of conferees immediately and get the word out right away, letting your members know what the deadline is for getting their messages to the conferees before the vote. For the same reasons that your group should be represented at a committee mark-up, it is very important to be present at the mark-up by conferees.

Action by the President

The president either signs a bill into law or vetoes it. If the president vetoes the bill, the veto can be overturned only by a two-thirds vote in both houses.

Your organization will usually know well in advance whether the president supports your legislation. If a veto is a possibility, your grassroots will have to be mobilized immediately after Congress passes the legislation, because the president is required to take action on a bill 10 days (not counting Sundays) after it is received from Congress. It takes strong grassroots support to enact legislation, and that support can be enormously influential in persuading an undecided president to sign.

If a bill is vetoed, both houses usually take action to override the veto within a few days. It will be important for you to know of a presidential veto within hours, if not minutes. Once again, your grassroots supporters should be contacted immediately and urged to get in touch with their senators and representatives, in support of a veto override. Often there will not be time for you to get an alert out to the field and letters back in from the grassroots, so you must be prepared to telephone, fax, and e-mail your grassroots supporters and have them phone their positions to members of Congress or take other action that is equally speedy.

Facts About Legislators and the Legislative Process

It is important to remember that all members of a legislature are not equal. For example, majority party members may be more helpful to you than minority members. Majority party members control the particular house of Congress, and its members are chairs of the committees. The chairs have considerable power over committees' decisions. Moreover, senior members may also be more helpful, since they often have significant influence over committees' decisions, and they are more likely to be appointed to conference committees, where key decisions are made. Finally, some members of a committee may be more active than others, for a variety of reasons, including

the impact that a committee's legislative agenda may have on legislators' home districts.

While it is important to understand the legislative process, the fact that it is a process run by people makes it also important to put yourself in legislators' shoes. (For an exceptionally lively description of the people, pulls, and pressures in Congress, see Resource D, by Doug Siglin.) Try to understand how you would respond if you were in their position and were being contacted by your organization. Remember that legislators have many votes on their minds and demands on their time. They cannot learn about each issue in the same depth as you know your issues. It is important to be patient with the legislator who does not seem to understand the program you are backing. If the legislator cannot help you on your issue this time, give him or her the benefit of the doubt. Don't take it personally. Maybe the legislator will be with you next time.

The federal government and many state governments provide detailed information on the legislative process. *Enactment of a Law* (1997) by Robert B. Dove, Parliamentarian of the U.S. Senate and *How Our Laws are Made* (1997) by Charles W. Johnson, House Parliamentarian provide very useful information about the legislative process in Congress, taking a bill step by step from introduction through enactment. It is important for the beginning lobbyist to know the basics of the process, so that he or she will know which questions to ask. Books on the legislative process can help, but it is often even more helpful to get information from people in the legislature. They can help you understand how the process works in practice, and they will probably feel complimented that you have come to them for direction. For example, it is crucial to know that few steps in the process are likely to be critical to the fate of your legislation. The person who will help you the most in knowing which steps are most important is almost always the legislator who has taken the lead on your bill, or that legislator's staff person.

Staff in Legislatures

Most senior staff members in legislatures, and even some who are not so senior, wield enormous behind-the-scenes power. The ability of your lobbyist to develop a good working relationship with the legislative staff person assigned to your bill is almost as important as your selection of the legislator who will lead your effort. Staff people can be very useful to your organization. They can help you (1) become familiar with the other members of the committee and their staffs, (2) know who among them should be targeted to support the bill early in the process, (3) know which legislators' staffs will help and which ones will not, (4) obtain regular updates on where committee members stand on your bill, (5) know what actions would be helpful from your grassroots and when, (6) show you how to get the most out of hearings on your measure, and (7) obtain information on how to get legislative-report language that strengthens your bill. They can also help you with much more. You, of course, will be developing information on key members of the legislature from other sources as well. By cross-checking that information with a legislative staff person who is taking the lead on your bill, you can greatly improve the targeting of all your efforts.

For your part, there are a number of ways in which you can be helpful to your legislative staff person in moving your legislation forward. You can offer to draft a statement that his or her boss can use in conducting hearings on your bill or in getting ready to speak on your measure before a group. After a committee votes favorably to move your bill out of committee, you can also offer to help develop draft language for the report on the legislation. A committee report includes information on the committee's findings and recommendations. The opportunity to draft such a statement helps you ensure that your group's views will be appropriately included. The key point is that you should be alert to the many ways in which you can offer to help the legislative staff person move your bill, by offering to take on some of the necessary writing or other staff work.

Over time, you will get a sense of how much the staff person will be willing to help. Because of the extraordinary number of hours they may spend on a measure, staff people often develop commitment to the legislation that is even greater than their bosses' commitment. Such commitment can help significantly in moving your legislation. Keep in mind, however, that the legislator has the final say and that keeping his or her commitment strong is crucial. Regardless of how strongly a staff person feels about your bill, he or she won't be able to win the day for you if the legislator is willing to trade your bill for another.

You will want to find a way of recognizing staff people who have been especially helpful. Presenting a plaque, or offering similar recognition, before an appropriate group is one way. But remember that the most important public recognition should always go to the legislator.

Perhaps it goes without saying that trust is absolutely central to building a strong relationship with staff people. Keeping commitments to staff people to hold information in confidence is crucial, as difficult as it may be sometimes. Not only is it right to do so, but you won't get a second chance if you slip up.

Most nonprofits that lobby don't start by learning the legislative process, nor should they. Most begin by doing what they already know how to do with great effectiveness. They write letters, they telephone, or perhaps they even visit their legislators, to let lawmakers know how particular legislative proposals will affect their organizations' services. It's not that knowing the lobbying process isn't helpful; someone in your organization should know at least a few of the basics. It's important, however, not to get entangled by trying to achieve complete mastery of the labyrinthine legislative process before you take action. Keep your eye on the target and on the thing that nonprofits do best: telling your organization's story effectively to your legislators. If some try to convince you that you must master all the intricacies of the legislative process before taking action on legislation, remind them that Irving Berlin never stopped to learn to read or write music.

If you are new to lobbying, remember that there is no one right or wrong way to lobby. There are as many ways to lobby as there are people who do it. Remember, too, that you won't learn to lobby by reading this book or any other. You learn to do it by doing it.

Lobbying the Administration

Actions of the executive branch of government, such as the issuing of regulations that spell out the intent of legislation, can profoundly affect programs supported by nonprofits. It is possible for an administration at any level of government to modify legislation so greatly that truth is lent to the old adage, "What the legislature gives through legislation, the administration takes away through regulation."

Often, the regulations proposed by an executive agency will change the original purposes of legislation so greatly that nonprofits must fight every bit as hard to change the regulations as they did to enact the measure in the first place. For example, the regulations proposed in late 1986 by the IRS to implement the 1976 lobby law were so restrictive and ambiguous that they threatened to end lobbying by most nonprofits. Only after a grueling four-month battle, in which nonprofits lobbied administration officials and enlisted the support of Congress, did the IRS agree to consider drafting new regulations. Superb lobbying regulations governing the 1976 law were ultimately issued by the IRS in 1990.

Nonprofits may lobby an administration for a variety of reasons: seeking changes in regulations, encouraging an administration to propose legislation or appropriations, or urging an administration to support a measure being considered by a legislature. Regardless of the reasons, the lobbying techniques, including the involvement of legislative volunteer networks, are very similar to those used in lobbying a legislature, and they are neither difficult nor complex.

Anyone who can write a letter or make a telephone call can effectively lobby an administration for a policy change, through contacting the administration directly or through contacting members of the legislature and urging them to ask the administration to support the measure.

Staff people in the executive branch are not always responsive to lobbying by nonprofits. For example, the staff responsible for drafting IRS regulations and other policies are often civil service personnel, not political appointees. Therefore, they are not very vulnerable to pressures from the grassroots. Often, however, staff members are open to reason when they are presented with arguments about how proposed regulations will negatively affect programs supported by the nonprofits. If the people in an executive agency who are ultimately responsible for regulations are not willing to make changes, then nonprofits have to find other avenues to get the administration to make modifications.

Enlisting the Help of the Legislature

Success in changing proposed regulations usually requires your lobbying the executive (president, governor, mayor) and/or the heads of executive departments or agencies who are *appointed* by the chief executive and have reason to be more responsive to grassroots pressures, such as those from legislative networks. At the federal level, effective lobbying of the administration almost always involves enlisting the help of members of Congress.

Members of Congress resent having their legislation modified by regulations in ways that they or their constituents think are not consistent with original legislative intent. Enlisting the support of the chair and other members of the appropriate legislative committee can be critically important in mobilizing support for modifying the regulations. At the same time, staff people in the executive agency that has drafted the regulations are interested in maintaining good relationships with the chair and other members of the committee responsible for enacting the legislation. After all, committee members usually have the power to affect the well-being—often including the appropriations—of the agency that developed the regulations. Enlisting large numbers of other legislators can also help greatly in moving the administration to modify or drop proposed regulations. In any case, the point is that legislators have much more power than nonprofits do to influence an administration. By all means, enlist them in your efforts. In the 1987 battle with the IRS over the regulations governing lobbying by nonprofits, it was finally the involvement of Senators Moynihan (D-NY), Packwood (R-OR), DeConcini (D-AZ), and D'Amato (R-NY) and of Congressmen Rostenkowski (D-IL), Rangel (D-NY), and Vander Jagt (R-MN)—all key members of committees that have jurisdiction over the IRS or authority for its appropriations—that played the pivotal role in getting the agency to reconsider its regulations.

If you have enlisted the support of a key legislator to help you get an administration to change proposed regulations, make a special effort to develop a good working relationship with the legislator's congressional staff person. Staff people know that nonprofits can help mobilize constituents to support their bosses' efforts. They play a pivotal, behind-the-scenes role in providing up-to-the minute information, circulating "Dear Colleague" letters, assisting with hearings, and making their bosses available to meet with nonprofits as an encouragement to lobbying efforts. Keep in mind that senior staff people almost always know what actions by members of Congress will have the greatest impact on the administration. Look to them for suggestions regarding strategy.

Getting the Press's Support

Getting press support for your position, and press criticism of the government's position, can also have an enormous impact. News stories, editorials, op-ed pieces, letters to the editor in support of your position on regulations or other administrative initiatives—all of these will help get the attention of any administration. Simply getting press coverage will not win your issue. But press coverage, along with grassroots lobbying, lobbying of the administration by influential members of your nonprofit, and most important, the support of legislators, will often generate the strength you need for the change you seek.

3

Effective Communications: The Key to Mobilizing Your Lobbying Strength

Unlike many other lobbying groups, a nonprofit organization's power does not come from contributions to a legislator's campaign (that's prohibited). It comes from well-informed members[1] who recognize the value of encouraging legislators to support the nonprofit's legislative issues. While they cannot contribute dollars to a legislator, nonprofits are nevertheless important to him or her because they constitute an important force in the community by virtue of the quality and the number of the members, as well as the importance of the group's mission. Legislators are particularly sensitive to groups from their home districts, since such groups are composed of the legislator's constituents, and their members go to the polls. The key question is how you can communicate with your organization's members so that they will contact their legislators on behalf of the group's concerns.

Many nonprofits rely completely on written communications to move their members to action. They fail to recognize that if written communications were followed up with telephone calls, the organization would greatly multiply the number of contacts its members make

with legislators. Most of us find it all too easy to put aside written communications that request us to take action, especially if the action involves writing a letter or calling a legislator. Our intentions are good; we plan to do it in a day or two, but somehow that day never comes. We have to give time and thought to the communication, and there are other pressing demands on our time. If we are called, however—if there is a person on the other end of the line urging us to act on the request—we are much more likely to do it.

Telephone follow-up is time-consuming and can be costly, but the increased contacts repay the investment of time and money. Moreover, those who phone always receive valuable information from the key volunteers and other organization representatives to whom they are speaking, through the give-and-take of a conversation. Furthermore, those who make the calls almost always find the process itself energizing, given the camaraderie that develops between the callers and those who are being asked to make the contacts.

Some organizations cut the costs of telephoning by setting up a telephone tree, whereby one person calls five people, and each of those five calls five more, and so on. Regardless of how you do it, it is critically important that you make calls to urge response to your action alerts. You may be inclined to mail your alert to members and others, hoping that will be enough to generate the action you want. Resist that impulse. Telephoning is hard work, but it often makes the difference between success and failure.

In any communication with your members, accuracy counts. If a member of your organization uses inaccurate

---

[1] The term "members" principally refers to individuals who have membership in a nonprofit but it may also include other individuals or organizations affiliated with the nonprofit.

information that he/she received from you when he/she communicates with a legislator, everyone loses. The legislator loses because accuracy is critically important to all that he or she does. Your group's member loses credibility with the legislator, and you lose credibility with your member. If you inadvertently send inaccurate information to your members, always correct it as quickly as possible, painful as that may be.

It is difficult but important to try to keep your legislative alert (your explanation of the issue and the action needed) to one sheet, front and back. If you must send more information, attach supplemental briefing materials and provide an executive summary of the materials. Nothing dampens a contact person's enthusiasm more quickly than receiving a legislative alert that calls for quick action but obliges the recipient to wade through four or five pages to get the necessary information. Be certain that your first paragraph tells the reader what the issue is and what action is needed, and clearly label the main messages in the alert. You will have to work at it, but you risk losing the reader if he or she doesn't get the main message first.

Don't use legislative jargon in your alert. It may take a few more words to convey what a mark-up is, but why use the term if you're not absolutely certain that all your readers know that a mark-up is a committee making its final changes in legislation?

Keep your alert self-contained, so that the reader doesn't have to refer to an earlier alert (they have probably discarded it). Don't make assumptions about how much your readers know from your past

communications with them. In the heat of a key legislative fight, you are living with the issue 24 hours a day, but they are not. They cannot make an intelligent contact if your alert does not provide adequate background information, so provide the basic details even though it may be redundant for some readers.

Just to be doubly certain that your alert is clear, ask several others in your office, who are not as close to the issue as you are, to read it for clarity. If you are fortunate enough to have volunteers, they can be particularly helpful, because they probably will be relatively new to the subject and therefore can read the alert for clarity from an outsider's point of view.

Be certain that your communications are mailed soon enough for your members to contact their legislators. Nothing makes your organization look worse (to say nothing of hurting your cause) than mailing your alert too late for action. It is important to know how quickly mail usually reaches your members. If you have any doubt about the time necessary to reach people by mail, use the telephone, or send faxes or e-mail to get your message to your members.

Newer Communications Technologies for Mobilizing Support

The past decade has brought huge changes in communications technologies that hold great potential for nonprofits' advocacy. Electronic mail, websites, faxes, and telephone routing systems allowing calls to members of Congress have come into their own in the past ten years, some within the past two, and provide an effective way for nonprofits to quickly mobilize their members for action on legislation. Each has strengths and limitations: e-mail is useful for helping to organize a lobbying campaign but may not be as useful in communicating with legislators; websites may be useful for making important information available but require an individual to take time to search, find, and have the information printed; telephone calls are very valuable in communicating with legislators because of the personal touch but are often difficult to mobilize in large numbers.

There are two ways in which newer technologies can be useful tools to nonprofits. They can be used to help organize lobbying campaigns or to educate the public about issues. They can also be used to directly communicate with or lobby legislators. On this last point, it's important to note that the final word is not yet in on the technologies' value as a tool for direct communications with legislators. New survey data (OMB Watch, June 1998) seems to show that fax is increasingly accepted as a means for communicating with Congress; six years ago it was not perceived as such (Burson-Marsteller, 1992). Similarly, e-mail today is not rated very highly as a useful form of communication by congressional offices, but it is being used increasingly and may become more accepted. Without doubt the best forms of communication remain letters (including faxed letters), calls, and personal visits.

The value of the new technologies in communicating with an organization's members has been demonstrated repeatedly in numerous successful advocacy efforts, such as recent efforts to stop the Istook initiatives in Congress to curtail nonprofit lobbying, to ban land mines, and to set aside 1.7 million acres of federal land in Utah as a national monument. Skilled use of new technologies holds real promise for nonprofits, for several reasons. First, it provides a quick and inexpensive means of mobilizing a nonprofit's members and other groups interested in an issue. Often legislative issues move at a very fast pace; e-mail allows a nonprofit to communicate with its members to keep them up-to-the-minute and engaged in the policy debate in a manner that never before existed. Second, it promises to level the playing field a bit between nonprofits and those groups that are permitted to contribute financially to candidates for public office. While nonprofits can't contribute to candidates' campaigns or to parties, they do have an important advantage over for-profits. Nonprofits usually have large cadres of people at the grassroots interested in their causes. The new technologies now make it possible to reach those people almost instantaneously, at relatively modest cost, to urge them to contact legislators. Third, it creates new ways of educating members and the public about issues without significant cost. Instead of the expense (and time) for mailings, nonprofits that have websites can now make information available through their sites, allowing their members and the public to learn about an issue—and possibly get more involved.

New technologies can greatly strengthen nonprofits' lobbying, but more traditional communications such as personal letters, telephone calls, and visits with legislators remain the most important means, by far, of getting your message across to legislators. It is important, however, for staff of nonprofits to develop at least basic skills in receiving and sending information via the new technologies. Following is a brief summary of these technologies and how nonprofits are putting them to use.

E-mail

E-mail has an enormous advantage over other means of communication because it creates a new type of interactivity among nonprofits and members of a nonprofit. With e-mail—and "listservers," which are e-mail discussion groups—people do not need to get together or arrange a conference call at the same time in order to discuss issues. Moreover, the communications can be sent and received nearly instantaneously and the recipient may in-turn e-mail the information to others whom he or she knows are interested in the issue—and each of those might send it to others, resulting in rapid and huge cumulative outreach and impact.

While e-mail holds great promise as a means of organizing a nonprofit's grassroots, it's important to know that members of Congress have not yet fully incorporated ways to respond to e-mail that they receive despite the fact that these offices are receiving a lot of e-mail (see Chapter 4).

Websites

The World-Wide Web, like e-mail, involves using the Internet. Like e-mail, the Web allows nonprofits to share information worldwide at low cost. Unlike e-mail, which a member of a nonprofit can automatically receive when he or she opens their e-mail software, the Web requires the individual to go "visit" or research for information. In other words, the Web requires the person to actively search for things, making it less useful in some lobbying campaigns where

information must be distributed very quickly. On the other hand, the Web provides access to detailed information that allows a "one stop" location for people to find out what is happening on a particular issue. In the past, the Web required significant and costly computer resources, with the result that few nonprofits or their members had access. However, with computer costs dropping dramatically, the Web has become more widely available.

A website can be used in multiple ways. For example, a nonprofit can post legislative updates or analyses of issues. These materials are available to anyone visiting the website. Combined with widely accessible search engines, such as Yahoo and Alta Vista, your website will be available to a very wide audience. A person searching for a specific issue through a search engine may then link to your website. Thus, the Web becomes a vast library for people around the world.

The website can also be used to send e-mail or faxes directly to legislative offices. A nonprofit can have an e-mail link to its legislator (if the office has e-mail) directly from the website. For statewide or national nonprofits, there can be e-mail links to state delegations or to everyone in Congress who has e-mail. In addition to e-mail links, the website can provide a fax link to the legislative office. This might be useful because e-mail still is not as widely used as faxes.

Because websites are passive rather than active tools for information dissemination, it is important to pay attention to marketing your website. Good marketing is very important because there are millions of websites and their growth has been exponential. Some groups are using e-mail to market their website. One nonprofit dramatically increased its outreach via the Web by advertising its website in selected magazines, periodicals, and other places nationwide to get the attention of those interested in their cause. Website visitors were urged to send their names and addresses to that organization's action update mailing list, which enabled the group to compile e-mail addresses of 30,000 supporters. The organization's Washington coordinator can now, at the touch of a key, ask everyone on the list to write or call their legislators.

Websites permit groups with modest budgets to alert their members with minimal charge through the Internet. In short, a website can provide all that is needed for a visitor to a site to send a personalized e-mail letter to a legislator. Remember, however, that some members of Congress do not have e-mail, and those that do generally rank it below other means of communication as a tool to get a message across.

Faxes

Many organizations send faxes to get their messages on legislation out quickly to their members when fast action is required. More nonprofits have fax machines than e-mail, so faxes, including broadcast faxes, are used more extensively than e-mail for legislative alerts. Nonprofits sometimes find that some of their members can receive only faxes, while others are limited to receiving only e-mail. In that situation, the sending nonprofit usually develops the capacity to send both e-mail and faxes.

Broadcast faxes permit an organization to send a fax quickly to literally hundreds of individuals either through the nonprofit's office or through a commercial faxing company. A nonprofit may, for example, key 50 numbers into their own fax machine and have the capacity to broadcast fax regularly to all 50 by putting the material to be faxed through the fax machine just one time. Nonprofits usually turn to commercial firms for faxes to larger numbers of recipients. A fax may be sent to literally thousands of recipients by electronically sending a fax list to a commercial fax company. That company can rapidly disseminate your fax at reasonable rates.

The quality of fax machines has improved substantially, so even information that has been refaxed several times usually is still legible. But neither faxed nor e-mailed material comes close to matching materials sent by postal mail in terms of legibility, attractiveness, and effectiveness. If postal mail will get your message out in sufficient time for the recipient to take action, it's still the preferred way of sending alerts. As with e-mail, Congressional offices were somewhat slow to welcome faxes but a faxed letter is acceptable.

Telephone Routing Systems

While many nonprofits are familiar with the availability of toll free telephone numbers, most do not know about how to link such services with routing calls to legislative offices. Using a toll free telephone number, a nonprofit can produce a barrage of calls to legislators if the number is advertised widely to interested groups. Typically, the caller to the toll free number receives a brief message on the issue and then is provided access to his or her legislator through various automated means. These automated systems can operate by allowing the caller to be connected directly to the legislator's office or by sending a form fax letter. The cost to arrange for these telephone routing systems is approximately $500 and the charge per minute might range from 35¢ to 50¢ (1998 estimated costs).

The nonprofit may arrange a telephone routing system where the organization pays for the call, or the individual making the call may be billed. Since personal telephone calls are considered a powerful way of communicating with legislators, it makes sense to encourage the use of a toll free telephone routing system. Moreover, the nonprofit could advertise the availability of the telephone routing system through e-mail and website.

Zip Code Matching

New software technology allows an organization to automatically match individuals or groups with their legislators at the click of a button. This is done by matching the zip code with a legislative district. Some programs require nine-digit zip codes to ensure accuracy, while other programs can insert the four-digit zip code extension through a verification of the address.

Zip code matching permits you to quickly contact all of your contacts in legislative districts of key members of the legislature whose votes are needed to support a legislative initiative. The cost of each match between a legislator and a person in the legislative district varies from about 15¢ to 25¢ (1998 estimate), with a minimum total expenditure of $950.

Zip code matching can also be used to allow your members to contact the correct legislator on an issue. (Sometimes members are not certain of the names of their legislators.) This zip code matching software can be employed through your website or through your telephone routing system discussed above.

What's the Best Technology to Use?

There will always be debate about the value of newer technologies in lobbying campaigns. Although the personal form of communication is always the best, the bottom line is that a successful lobby campaign today needs to incorporate multiple approaches to educating and mobilizing members and communicating with legislators.

Feedback and Records

Encourage your members always to send you copies of any correspondence that they have received from legislators. Nonprofits' members are sometimes slow to provide their information, but encourage them to do so. All replies, even those that are noncommital, tell you something about the legislator's position.

If you are seeking cosponsors for your legislation, regularly send your members a list of all legislators and indicate who has already signed on. Your members will check the list to see if their legislators are cosponsors and will know whether they need to get in touch with them. Regular updates also keep your members involved by showing them the results of their efforts.

Tallies of Support

It is very important to keep a confidential support tally that gives your judgments regarding legislators' positions. This list could be coded as follows:

S = supports
LTS = leaning toward support
U = undecided
LAS = leaning against support
A = against

It is also important to remember that these judgments are often subjective, since they are pieced together from information that may have a variety of sources. Such a list should not be sent out to your members. A person who sees that her legislator is leaning against support of your measure may write to the legislator and ask why he or she is not supporting it, even though the "leaning against" designation is simply a judgment that you made, and it may not be altogether accurate. The legislator probably will be unhappy, to say the least, about receiving a communication that does not accurately reflect his or her position. This misunderstanding may damage the relationship between your member and the legislator, and between your member and you. Even though such a list must be treated with caution, it can still be very important to your group's leaders and to the legislator who is leading the effort on your measure. The legislator will need regular updates of your assessment of support for the measure. On the basis of the tally, you can selectively urge your members to make special contacts with legislators who are not supportive, taking care to communicate those legislators' positions in such a way that your volunteers can act without jeopardizing relationships.

Frequency of Alerts

Legislative alerts should be sent out as often as necessary, which may mean three times in one month and not at all for the next several months. Some nonprofits send out government relations updates at designated times each month, even if there is little to report. There are those who argue that sending a government relations update on a regular schedule develops a readership, but that is not likely to happen if you are stretching to fill up the space. You will soon lose your readers' interest and their possible supportive actions unless you are reporting something worthy of their time.

Staying with the Process

Major legislative changes often take many years to achieve, and it is sometimes difficult to keep members motivated for that long. It is important to be candid from the start about the time that may be required. You should also emphasize that persistence ranks close to the top, if it is not at the top, of any list of attributes essential to a successful legislative effort. There's no magic to success, just perseverance and hard work.

4

How to Communicate Effectively with Legislators

There have been a number of studies on which communications help most in influencing a legislator's point of view, but keep in mind that there is more than one way to make your communication count. The most effective method will be the one that, over time, works best for your group. Personal visits, thoughtful letters from constituents, site visits (where a legislator sees first-hand the needs your group is trying to meet), and telephone calls from constituents whom the legislator respects—all of these can be highly effective. On balance, a personal visit from an influential constituent is clearly better than a letter or a phone call from the same constituent, and one site visit would probably be better than ten personal visits or one-hundred letters or phone calls. You will develop your own sense of what works best. Your own experience will be a far better guide than any study, although studies can provide some useful general direction for your work.

A comprehensive study by Burson-Marsteller (1992) provides important information about which sources of communications congressional staff rated as most effective. Staff people's views are important because of the enormous influence that staffers exert on the members of Congress for whom they work. There were several major findings in the study and they are remarkably similar to earlier studies. First, spontaneous, individually composed letters from constituents were seen as the most effective way of communicating with congressional decision makers. These letters received more attention than any other form of written communication. Office visits by constituents rank a very close second, followed by articles in state and congressional district newspapers and telephone calls from opinion leaders in the state and congressional district. (For a complete listing of the attention congressional staffs give to selected communications and the comparative frequency of such communications see Table 1, p. 25)

The Burson-Marsteller report highlights the following points:

- Congressional offices pay more attention to personal communications from constituents than any other source. In fact, an average of 75 percent of offices pay a great deal or quite a bit of attention to communications from constituents.

- The best way to gain the attention of congressional staffs is to contact them personally, either by letter, telephone call, or office visit. Personal letters, whether prompted or not, are the most effective form of communication. Indeed, 90 percent of offices pay a great deal or quite a bit of attention to spontaneous mail from constituents.

- Congressional offices report a greater volume of incoming communications in 1991 than they did in the survey conducted 10 years ago. This is true for over 80 percent of the types of communications tested in this survey.

- State and district newspapers have become more important over the past decade as a mechanism by which to communicate positions to members of Congress. An average of almost half (49 percent) of the congressional offices say they pay a great deal or quite a bit of attention to print media and the largest increases in frequency all involved state and district newspapers.
- The increasing number of communications flowing into congressional offices means staff members are more pressed than ever to address the volume. This puts more pressure on those who communicate with Congress to keep their messages short and informative.
- Issue advertising in national daily newspapers and communicating by fax and videotape receive less attention than other types of communication.

The consensus among congressional staff in the 170 offices contacted was that the following "rules" are important in effective communications:

- **Keep it local.** The local constituency is, obviously, most important to the member of Congress. In establishing priorities in communications, this fact is more decisive than any other.
- **Keep it personal.** Personal forms of communication indicate a greater amount of effort, and the more obvious the effort, the more seriously the communication is taken.
- **Keep it concise.** Given the busy nature of congressional offices, the more concise the communication, the more likely it is to receive attention.
- **Put it in writing.** Hard copy provides a readily available record in the office that can be used whenever a staff member addresses the issue.

Letter writing, the lobbying technique most used by nonprofits, ranks right at the top in the survey. Regardless of which means of communication you use, there are a few general guidelines and tips that will help you make your point with legislators.

Perhaps the most important thing you need to know is your subject. What is the substance of the legislation? Why is it important? What will happen if it passes? What will be the consequences if it fails? How much will it cost? Most important, what will be the impact of the legislation on the legislator's constituents? It is particularly helpful to give an illustration or two of how the problem will affect the legislator's district, but don't feel that you have to become an expert on the subject before you make the communication. Just be sure of the facts that you report, and build your communication around them.

It helps to know at least a little about your legislator, and Congressional Quarterly's *Politics in America, 1998, 105th Congress*, is one good source of detailed information on the individual members of Congress, including positions they have taken, their interest group rating, and their education, occupation, and so on. However, don't let any lack of detailed knowledge about your legislators

Table 1. Highest-Ranked Sources of Communication

Rank	Method	1991 Great Deal/Quite A Bit (%)	1991 Very Frequently/Often (%)
1.	Spontaneous letters from constituents	90	94
2.	Office visits from constituents	91	86
3.	Articles in state/district newspapers	86	96
4.	Telephone calls from opinion leaders in the state/district	85	58
5.	Congressional Research Service	82	79
6.	Telephone calls from constituents	81	88
7.	Office visits from chief executive officers of businesses in the state/district	81	36
8.	Editorials in state/district newspapers	77	84
9.	Office visits from delegations from interest groups, including constituents	75	74
10.	Telephone calls from state-elected or party officials	73	38
11.	Opinion or op-ed pieces in state/district newspapers	71	85
12.	Office visits from long-standing friends or contacts with an interest	69	53
13.	Spontaneous mail from state-elected or party officials	65	29
14.	Telephone calls from friends or contacts with interest	64	59
15.	News programs on TV stations in the state/district	54	41
16.	Articles in major daily newspapers	51	77
17.	Telephone calls from the executive branch	46	20
18.	National TV news	45	74
19.	News programs on radio stations in the state/district	39	31
20.	Editorials in major daily newspapers	34	73
21.	Orchestrated mail from constituents	34	79
22.	Office visits by company Washington representatives	33	69
23.	Radio talk shows in the state/district	31	29
24.	Media-sponsored public opinion polls	30	41
25.	Office visits from lobbyists	28	84
26.	Letters to the editor in major daily newspapers	26	49
27.	Office visits from representatives of trade associations	25	63
28.	Articles in national news magazines	25	66
29.	Opinion or op-ed columns in national news magazines	24	51
30.	Spontaneous mail from interest groups	23	62
31.	Issue ads on TV stations in the state/district	21	10
32.	Privately-sponsored public opinion polls	20	21
33.	Orchestrated mail from members of interest groups	16	80
34.	Petition papers from interest groups	16	37
35.	Issue ads in state/district newspapers	16	12
36.	Issue ads on radio stations in state/district	15	6
37.	Office visits from well-known personalities with an interest	14	7
38.	Position papers from regulatory and executive agencies	14	40
39.	Communications with think tanks	13	52
40.	Economic studies conducted by independent consultants	12	22
41.	Commentaries on network or syndicated TV programs	12	34
42.	Telephone calls from well-known personalities with an interest	10	6
43.	Telephone calls from members of interest groups	9	53
44.	Office visits by delegations from interest groups, not including constituents	8	43

Source: Adapted from Burson-Marsteller (1992).

stand in your way. Legislators pay attention to well-presented positions by constituents regardless of whether the presenters tie in the points they are making with personal knowledge about legislators.

In all communications, whether by phone calls, letters, or personal meetings, it is important to be accurate, brief, clear, and timely, as already discussed. No matter how much you will sometimes want to, never become angry or argumentative with your legislator about his or her failure to support your position. You will almost certainly have to go back to that same legislator sometime in the future. If you have strained your relationship by getting angry—no matter how much you may have been justified in doing so—chances are that you won't get through the door. If you do, your information may be largely discounted.

In addition to these general guidelines, there are more specific tips that may help you. Since these tips cover far more information than you will need, just skim through them, see what fits for you, and ignore the rest.

Letters

Nonprofit organizations rely greatly on mail campaigns to persuade legislators to support positions. Whether you are organizing a mail campaign or writing just one letter from your organization, it is important to keep in mind that the competition is stiff. More than 200,000,000 pieces of mail are sent to Congress each year, so give careful thought to your letter. (Table 2 shows proper forms of address to be used with various state and federal officials.)

If you know the legislator, make that clear in the first paragraph. This will alert the person opening the mail to give the letter special attention. By all means, use the legislator's first name if you have established that kind of relationship, and sign it with your first name.

Some legislators downgrade the importance of a letter if they think it has been motivated by an organization as part of a campaign so letters on plain stationery or on your personal or business letterhead may get greater attention than a letter on your nonprofit's letterhead. Do, however, mention your nonprofit group if you are fairly certain that it will strengthen the impact of your letter.

Handwritten letters are fine, as long as they are legible. They often get more attention than typed letters. (Legislators know that a machine cannot produce a handwritten letter.)

Keep your letter to one page. Put it in your own words, avoid bold words or jargon, and use only those acronyms that you are very certain the legislator will know. Cover only one issue per letter. In the first paragraph, ask for the action that you want your legislator to take. Send enclosures if you think more information is needed. Relevant editorials and news stories from local papers in the legislator's district will get his or her attention. Identify the legislation clearly, with the bill number of the legislation if you know it, and sign your letter over your typed or printed name.

Table 2. Proper Forms of Address

Person Addressed		Salutation	Complimentary Close
President of the United States	The President The White House Washington, D.C. 20500	Dear Mr. President:	Sincerely yours,
U.S. Senator	The Honorable _____ United States Senate Washington, D.C. 20510	Dear Senator _____:	Sincerely yours,
U.S. Representative	The Honorable _____ United States House of Representatives Washington, D.C. 20515	Dear Mr./Ms. _____:	Sincerely yours,
	The Honorable _____ Governor of _____	Dear Governor _____:	Sincerely yours,
	The Honorable _____ House of Representatives State Capitol	Dear Mr./Ms. _____:	Sincerely yours,
	The Honorable _____ The State Senate State Capitol	Dear Senator _____:	Sincerely yours,

Ask the legislator to reply, and ask very directly whether he or she will support your position. Legislators are masters of nonreplies—that is, letters that avoid giving you their positions. To smoke out his or her position, be as direct as possible while still being courteous. Like everyone else, legislators dislike a threatening tone. Chances are excellent that your legislator will be very aware of the political fallout of not voting for your proposal, and so it serves no useful purpose to even hint about it. Keep in mind the old saying that you catch more flies with honey than you do with vinegar.

Be certain that the legislator's name is spelled correctly and that the address is right. Envelopes get detached, so put your return address on the letter. Be certain that your legislator receives the letter before the vote.

Thank the legislator. Legislative staffers repeatedly say that legislators seldom receive thanks. Sending your thanks is the right thing to do and is a great way to strengthen a relationship. But also write to let the legislator know if you disapprove of the way he or she has voted. That will get attention, too.

Provide copies of any replies you receive to the leaders and government relations committee of your nonprofit. It is useful to keep them up-to-date on where the legislator stands and on whether to keep pressure on him or her.

Don't overstate your nonprofit's influence; it will only detract from your message. Do let your legislator know the size and mission of your group, however. Legislators are very aware of how much attention to pay to almost every group in their districts, so don't overstate—or understate. Just give the facts.

Send letters only to your own legislator, unless you are the president of a group with members from other legislative districts. Even then, it is well to keep in mind that legislators tend to pay only limited attention to mail from outside their districts.

There have been mixed reviews of postcards, sample letters, and similar communications produced in centrally organized efforts to mobilize grassroots support on issues. Some discount the impact of postcards and "canned" letters. Others hold that they can be helpful. As Common Cause advises, any letter is better than none. That's still good advice.

If you are part of a coalition (see Chapter 6) and most of the coalition members already have sent letters regarding the legislative issue your group is tackling, you may want to take two additional steps: 1) Compose a sign-on letter that all members of the coalition, and others, will sign and send it to all members of the legislative body addressing your issue; 2) have each coalition member send a support letter with a "Dear Legislator" salutation to the coalition leader, who in turn will send all of the letters in one packet to the legislative body. Both are helpful in supplementing personal letters but they should not be seen as a replacement for them.

Personal Visits

Personal meetings with constituents are very highly ranked among effective ways of communicating with legislators. The first time you meet your legislator face to face, you may be nervous; it would be unusual if you were not. Keep in mind, however, that legislators are almost always very eager to win your support. They want to put their best foot forward with their constituents, and they are sincerely interested in getting their constituents' views on legislation. Remember that you are the expert on the subject—you have information that the legislator needs. Legislators and their staff people repeatedly say that the information nonprofits provide is important to their decisions, so don't feel that you are entering the legislator's office as a supplicant.

There will be many reasons why your group may want to meet with a legislator who is taking a leadership role on your bill. During the visit, don't miss the opportunity to seek advice on how your organization can be most helpful in developing support for your legislation. Remember that you will think of the bill you are supporting as your legislation, but the legislator will naturally consider it to be his or her bill and will have a number of ideas and suggestions to help you focus your efforts.

If you have decided to meet with your legislator, there are ways to help the meeting run smoothly. It is important to make an appointment, if at all possible. It is better to telephone than to write for the appointment, because calling makes it easier to find an acceptable date. It is also more difficult for the appointments' secretary to turn you down by telephone than by letter. It is always more effective if you as a constituent ask for an appointment, rather than having your organization's staff make that contact.

Legislators almost always do try to meet with their constituents. Don't turn down the opportunity to meet with a staffer, however, if it develops that the legislator cannot meet your schedule. In Congress, senior staff people wield considerable power and often are able to give more time and attention to issues than legislators can. Representatives and Senators maintain district offices, and meetings there can be particularly productive because legislators usually are less harried when they are home on weekends or during recesses.

It is acceptable to assemble a delegation for the meeting but remember that small meetings will allow for more detailed discussion of an issue, including frank comments from the legislator about the dilemma he or she faces in making choices on the issue. One delegate should be designated as the principal spokesperson. The group should meet at least briefly in advance, to orchestrate the visit. Be certain that there is agreement on the objectives to be accomplished in the meeting and on the points to be stressed.

Having more than one person presenting information permits a person who is not talking to the legislator to be ready to step in with the next key point, but don't overpower your legislator.

Present your views with conviction, but don't put him or her on the defensive.

You will probably know considerably more about your subject than your legislator does, so there is no reason to feel abashed. Legislators will welcome information and will particularly appreciate any anecdotes or illustrations that spell out what the impact will be on people in their legislative districts.

It helps to cover your issue from the legislator's perspective, tying it in with his or her past votes or interests. Listen attentively. Often, the legislator's opening discussion with you will give you clues about how to connect your issue with his or her concerns.

If you don't have the answer to a legislator's question, say so. Don't bluff. Tell the legislator that you will provide the information, and then be certain that you do.

Give responses to arguments that you know your opposition will raise, but don't degrade your opponents. They believe in their cause as strongly as you believe in yours. It is important to provide information, both orally and in a fact sheet that you leave with the legislator. Be certain that it includes a brief description of your issue, why it is important to your organization, and the action that you want the legislator to take. Give a copy of the fact sheet to the legislative aide as well. The aide may be your principal contact in the future, so be certain to strengthen that contact during the visit.

After the visit, write a letter of thanks to the legislator. Remind him or her of any agreements reached, and provide any information that you promised.

Testimony

Testimony ranks low on the list of effective ways to communicate with legislators, but it is important to know how to give it. Legislative bodies call for public hearings for a number of reasons. They may be held to inform the public about issues or to get the information they need in helping to draft laws or in finding out whether a law is needed. Hearings may also be scheduled as "window dressing" for decisions that have already been made.

At the very least, providing testimony—even when it is given in hearings of questionable value—serves the useful purpose of requiring a group to develop a fairly comprehensive statement of its position. Sound testimony can help to establish your organization as an authority in your field. It can also provide useful quotations for speeches and publications. In that way, testimony can be helpful to a nonprofit, even if hearings are perfunctory. In deciding whether to testify, remember that a decision against testifying sends a message to the legislators that your organization is not interested or, worse, that you have reasons to avoid questions on the subject.

If you are planning to present testimony, keep your statement brief, and always provide a one-page summary as the initial page of your written testimony. Legislators usually don't read testimony, and staffers often only scan it. Providing a summary helps ensure that your main points will be noted. Most legislative bodies have format requirements for testimony, including the number of copies you should have and when they should be delivered to the committee. The cover page of your statement should include the legislative committee before which you are testifying; the name, title, and organization of the person testifying; and the date. A written request is almost always required from a person who wishes to testify before Congress.

At congressional hearings, witnesses are usually asked to keep oral statements to under five minutes, although a longer statement will be accepted for the record.

Oral statements should not be read word by word. They should be given as much as possible from brief outlines that permit presenters to maintain eye contact with committee members. If you can't answer a question, it is perfectly acceptable to say that you don't have the information but will get it for the committee immediately.

The quality of your organization's statement is important, but the skill of the presenter is equally important in making a favorable impression for your cause. Testimony should be presented by a high ranking well-informed volunteer or the chief staff officer or other senior staff of your group. You will want the person who will make the best presentation.

It is helpful to know in advance which committee members are likely to be present and whether they will be friendly. That information is often available from the staff of the legislator who supports your position. Plant questions with friendly legislators who you know will be at the hearing, so that you can get those questions and your answers into the public record. It is usually easy to do this by working with legislative staff members. If there will be witnesses unfriendly to your cause, anticipate the opposing arguments they will make, and provide responses to friendly legislators. You can also provide questions to friendly legislators, which they can raise with unfriendly witness, to make points for you.

You may get questions that seem hostile. It is perfectly acceptable to be direct in your responses, but always be courteous. If a legislator seems particularly hostile, make a special point of trying to see him or her later, or follow up your testimony with a letter that deals with the issues he or she has raised.

If your organization is working closely with the chair of the committee holding the hearings, it is acceptable to ask staffers if they would like to have your group draft the opening statement for the chair. Staff people often welcome such statements as a starting point for the drafts they ultimately present to chairpersons.

Finally, get other groups to sign on to your testimony if they are not planning to testify separately. Having several other organizations that are well known to legislators sign on to your testimony can significantly strengthen the impact of the statement.

Phone Calls

In just about every legislative campaign, there are times when it is crucial to have immediate contact from the grassroots. There is often less then 24 hours' notice before a key vote comes up in committee or even before a final vote in the legislature. Many nonprofits have a process for telephoning constituents at this critical point and urging calls to legislators. The fact that a legislator receives 20 or so calls on your nonprofit's issue just before a vote can make a difference.

You can reach any member of Congress by calling (202) 224-3121. Using that number is almost as fast as calling the Congressperson's office directly. Telephone calls to district offices of legislators are second best, especially if the vote is imminent. They achieve the objective of communicating your message, but there may be a crucial delay in a district office's reporting your call to the legislator, particularly if he or she is not in the district at the time.

When a vote is coming up, it may not be possible on short notice to talk by phone with your legislator, regardless of how well you know him or her. If you can't reach the legislator, ask for the legislative aide who is assigned to your issue. If you can't reach the aide, leave your message with the person who answered the phone. Legislative offices do keep count of the pro and con calls on issues, so at least be certain to leave your message. Keep your call brief. There will be little if any time to persuade. Your message can simply be two sentences, one asking for support and the other stating why. To help you make your point succinctly, you may want to write out your message and have it before you when you call.

If you want to get a last-minute message to the White House regarding your organization's views on a matter that the administration is considering, call the White House Comment Line at (202) 456-7639.

E-mail and Faxes

About 90 percent of offices that responded to a recent survey said they use e-mail and reported, on average, receiving about 200 e-mail letters a week. According to the Bonner and Associates—American University survey on Congressional use of the Internet, reported February 1998, e-mails received from outside the Congressional district are not considered politically relevant and most offices do not use e-mail to communicate with constituents. E-mail is not used as a means of keeping constituents informed or to respond to their inquiries. Instead, the majority of offices respond to constituent e-mail by sending a postal letter.

Also, e-mail is not used as a means of educating the public. Fully 85 percent of congressional offices reported e-mail was not used to send constituents updates, and 81 percent said they were not planning to do so in the future.

Despite the above, the majority of Congressional offices think e-mail is a good thing. They view it as quick and inexpensive in providing another avenue for constituents to keep their elected officials informed.

Another recent, but much smaller survey (June 1998) by OMB Watch tends to confirm that spontaneous letters, telephone calls, and personal presentations from constituents get the greatest attention from Congressional offices when considering policy positions. However, faxes and e-mail from constituents rank considerably higher than form letters, postcard campaigns, and petitions—although e-mail did not rank as highly as faxes. Interestingly, a 1992 Burson-Marsteller survey found faxes ranking very low as a useful form of communication with Congress. In fact, in 1992, some staff members found faxes offensive because "fax was meant for urgent materials," as one staffer said. These new findings might suggest that Congressional offices are becoming more accustomed to and accepting of faxes and are likely to become comfortable with e-mail as appropriate means of communication. One warning is that the e-mail and faxes must be personalized to be effective.

In the OMB Watch survey, 72 percent of respondents said that in considering a policy position, they paid "a great deal" or "quite a bit" of attention

to constituent communications in the form of telephone calls, but it is interesting that faxes generated the same high percentage response. Letters scored highest, at 83 percent, and e-mail lowest, at 59 percent, on the question regarding what communications Congressional offices pay "a great deal" or "quite a bit" of attention to when considering policy positions. While this information suggests that faxes and e-mail are becoming more acceptable, it's clear that postal letters continue to rank highest and clearly are much preferred by Congressional staff.

A majority of offices report that the use of the Internet and e-mail will increase in the next year, but the expansion is not expected to be an explosion. In short, while e-mail is growing in popularity in Congress, there is no evidence that it will replace postal mail—at least in the near future—as the most effective means of communicating with constituents.

Telegrams, Mailgrams, and Form Letters

Telegrams and mailgrams are less effective than personal letters or telephone calls, but they can help register last-minute opinions before a vote. It takes no more time, and perhaps less, to phone a legislator's office than to call in a telegram or a mailgram. Unless you have good reason not to, call the legislator directly instead of relying on a telegram or a mailgram. Form letters are better than nothing at all, but their volume must be huge to get attention.

Other Communications

The number of ways you can use to get your story across to legislators is almost endless. Here are some examples:

1. Invite your legislator to visit a facility that provides services to your clients, and describe how those services will be affected by his or her vote on your issue. Such a visit, which can be arranged for a time when the legislator will be in your district, is perhaps the most effective way of communicating a need.

2. Have a legislator speak at a public meeting sponsored by your organization. Legislators usually appreciate such opportunities, if there is a chance to speak before a fairly large audience or if the audience is composed of people whom the legislator is particularly interested in reaching.

3. Invite the legislator to meet your board of directors at the regular board meeting. You will probably know whether your legislator will want to attend. If you are uncertain, ask; there is nothing to lose.

4. Some believe in holding receptions on Capitol Hill for legislators. These may provide opportunities to meet legislators or their staffs. In Washington, however, it is awfully difficult to turn out a large group of legislators on Capitol Hill. You often get very junior aides or interns, especially if it's late in the afternoon and there is food.

5. Organize a Capitol Hill day, and invite members from throughout the area served by your group to participate. The arrangements are very time-consuming, and there is mixed opinion regarding this tactic's effectiveness. In my experience, however, this approach can be very helpful if participants are well briefed and if appointments with legislators are set up.

6. Arrange for a number of two-person volunteer teams to visit legislators at the Capitol. If these key volunteers are leaders of your organization, they may also profitably visit legislators from other districts. Appointments are always recommended but are critically important for people who are not constituents of legislators.

7. A breakfast for legislators at a convenient location in the capital may be well attended because it does not cut into legislators' usual workday. Legislators are more likely to attend if they are invited by constituents who will also be there. Many state and local groups routinely use breakfasts as a forum for educating legislators.

When you find it expedient to do so, publicize any meetings that a legislator has with your organization.

5

*"All politics is local," according
to former Speaker of the House
Thomas "Tip" O'Neill. That's why
effective lobbying by nonprofits
requires a legislative network.*

The central mission of a network
is empowerment—helping
people know how and when to
take action on issues important to them
and those they seek to serve. Legislative
networks are time consuming to organize.
They require thoughtful attention to
maintain, are not very glamorous, and are
therefore easy to neglect. But remember,
as John F. Kennedy said, "Things don't
just happen. They're made to happen."
That's what legislative networks do.

It is a well-known fact that
communications from the grassroots do
have an important impact on decisions in
any legislature. Legislative staff people
repeatedly emphasize that those back-
home contacts are often the determining
factor in how their bosses vote on an
issue. But somehow we tend to be slow to
believe this fact and slower still to act on
it. Well-informed contacts by nonprofit
volunteers are at the heart of almost every
successful legislative effort, and that
volunteer action is best mobilized
through a legislative network.

Each nonprofit's legislative network
is different from the next, because
nonprofits have vastly different
organizational structures. But all
legislative networks have one thing in
common: an organized, systematic means
of communicating on short notice with
network volunteers who have agreed to
contact their legislators on behalf of
legislation backed by the nonprofits.

To start, the network doesn't have to
be elaborate. It can consist of only one
network volunteer, in each of the key
legislative districts represented on the
committee(s) that will be considering
your bill. Later, according to need, the
network can be expanded to all the
districts represented on these committees
and, ultimately, to the whole legislature.
But don't worry about organizing a
network to cover all legislators at the
outset. Instead, concentrate on
establishing a sound network for those
key members of the legislature who will
have the greatest influence on the
outcome of your bill.

It is important that your network be
composed of volunteers, if at all possible,
rather than the paid staff members of a
nonprofit. If you select influential
volunteers, their contacts, in most cases,
will have a far greater impact on
legislators than will the contacts of staff
people. Because they are contributing
their time, volunteers are also often
perceived by legislators and their staffs to
have less monetary interest in outcomes,
and so their contacts have more
credibility.

To set up a network, you simply
need to make a list of those legislators
whom you want to contact, delineate the
geographical district covered by each
legislator, recruit volunteers who live in
the appropriate districts and have (or can
establish) relationships with those
legislators, and develop a means of

communicating quickly with all the members of your network.

The information that you will need about each legislator to pass on to your network volunteers will include his or her political party, address in the capital, address in the legislative district, and telephone number. If available, you will also want the names of legislative staff people who will be assigned to your issue. While it is not crucial, it is helpful to include information on how legislators have voted on past issues of concern to your organization. Biographical information also helps. If you want several pages of biographical information on a member of Congress, it is available in the latest edition of *Politics in America* (1998).

It is important to recruit network volunteers who really have a commitment to your issue and who have staying power. Since it often takes a number of years to pass major legislation, commitment is important. Even the best relationship with a legislator is of little value if a volunteer is not going to work aggressively to gain the legislator's support, or if he/she loses interest when your bill does not show quick movement in the legislature.

It helps to recruit network volunteers who are known to and respected by the legislators and who live in their districts. This is the first criterion. If a volunteer doesn't know a legislator, try to make certain that the volunteer does have the capacity for developing a strong relationship.

The best way to be certain that your network volunteer will be effective is to have firsthand knowledge of that person. That isn't always possible, but others whom you trust may know someone who

would be right for the job. You can also send a mailing to your members, asking for volunteers for the legislative network. Volunteers can be asked to provide information about the strength of their contacts with legislators. Initially, you may be less certain that volunteers recruited by mail will follow through effectively on their responsibilities, but your experience over time with this group will tell you whom you can count on and should retain.

The principal job of network volunteers is to contact legislators on behalf of your issues. Their second responsibility, equally important, is to mobilize support by others in their communities. In many cases, network volunteers will be active with local chapters of your organization or with other groups, whose members can be recruited to support your legislation. It is very important for network volunteers to know that, at the very minimum, they are responsible for contacting legislators and reporting to you on those contacts, but it will help greatly to strengthen your impact if volunteers also agree to recruit others.

To have impact, network volunteers have to be able to provide sound, timely information to their legislators. Most nonprofits send action alerts to their network volunteers to provide that information, and the most effective groups *always* follow up the alert with a telephone call.

Your ability to generate contacts will be greatly increased if you follow up your action alerts with telephone calls. Some groups set up telephone "trees," where one person calls five people who then call an additional five, and so on. Other nonprofits set up a telephone "bank" in their office, where volunteers and/or staff call all network volunteers directly. Others use a combination. The key is to find a method of telephoning that is as foolproof as possible in the sense of assuring that the calls are made. Without the calls, you will lose much of the impact of your action alerts. The temptation, because telephoning can be so time-consuming, is simply to send the action alert and then just hope for the best. Don't do it. Make the calls.

It is, of course, vital that the action alert arrive in time for the volunteers to write the letter or call the legislator prior to action on your bill. Don't depend on your nonprofit's newsletter or bulletin to get the action from your volunteers. First off, chances are that it will not reach the people in the field at the time when the information is needed, and, in any case, publications that cover a wide variety of issues of concern to the organization do not convey the same sense of urgency and importance that separate legislative action alerts do. However, your organization's newsletter or bulletin can provide an effective supplement to your action alerts by giving a general update on the progress of the legislation.

Your action alert should state in the first sentence or two what action is needed. Don't leave out key information because it was in past alerts; it might have been forgotten or the alert discarded. Urge network volunteers to include illustrative anecdotes or other specific information in their contacts with legislators that show firsthand how the legislator's constituents will be affected by the vote on your issue. Ask volunteers always to thank legislators for their vote. It is the right thing to do and the

legislator and the legislator's staff will remember it.

Most nonprofits have several groups within their memberships that they reach out to for legislative action. They have primary networks of volunteers specifically designated to contact particular legislators. Most organizations, however, consider their total memberships to be part of their legislative networks. On issues of major importance, they try to mobilize action on the part of all members. Boards of directors and key committees should also be considered special networks, to be turned to on selected occasions.

When working with smaller groups, such as your nonprofit's board, you should get information about which legislators the members may know personally and about the strength of those contacts. It is far more difficult to get this kind of information from every member of the organization, but some nonprofits have been able to do so by polling members.

Boards, committees, other groups in your organization and the total membership can increase your organization's legislative impact substantially. Before organizing other groups, however, be certain that your primary network is in place and working well.

Keeping Your Network Alive

Legislative networks often do not remain effective over time. Some nonprofits are not really convinced that networks are where the power to effect legislative change resides, or they realize it but do not understand how necessary commitment and hard work are in keeping a network alive and effective.

Once a network is in place, there is often an inclination to consider the job done and go on to other, more interesting activities, such as meetings with legislators or their staffs. But thinking about the network only when action is needed won't work. To remain strong, a legislative network needs to be asked regularly to take action. Members must be kept up-to-date on what's happening with their legislation, even when action isn't required, and they need to be thanked, regularly and thoughtfully, for their work.

I disagree with those who hold that networks should be asked to take action only once or twice a year, for fear of wearing them out. The reverse is true. Networks atrophy because they are too seldom called on to do anything. As a result, they get the unstated message that they are not needed. It is important to ask for action only when it is really needed, but on any major legislative issue, that will be more than once or twice a year.

You can take several steps, in addition to asking for action, that will help keep volunteers as part of the team. Most important is that they get regular brief updates on where the legislation stands. If you can, also invite your network's members to come to the capital and receive updates from the legislators leading your effort. They can make calls on their legislators while in the capital and meet with your group's top leaders.

Saying "thank you" is both right and important. Finding a way of saying it to a large group in a sincere way is difficult. Making telephone calls is one effective way of conveying special thanks that won't sound "canned." If it's worth your time to call network volunteers and urge them to take action on legislation, then it is certainly worth the time and expense to call them occasionally with updates and thanks. A letter sometimes conveys the message, although most volunteers recognize a mass-mailed letter produced by a computer, even if the letter is personally signed. You may want to express your thanks in a legislative alert, but make your thanks special by having the legislator who is leading your effort formulate the statement. (You can probably formulate the statement for the legislator and get it approved through your staff contact.) In addition, publicly state your volunteer leaders' names in your organization's newsletter or in a similar publication.

To find out whether your network is working, make inquiries of staff people who should be hearing from your grassroots. They will let you know how much they are hearing on your issue. If it turns out that some volunteers are not doing the job, it is important to thank them and find replacements.

Keeping Up-to-Date Information

One side benefit of calling network volunteers to action is that you turn up new information that can help you know how to target your future efforts. Be sure that the person telephoning the volunteers records any new information regarding legislators' positions. Equally important, also record any information that indicates how network volunteers are doing their jobs. Over time, you will develop a list of network volunteers who are especially responsive. They will become a select group that you will call fast, because they can be counted on to take quick action. Their responsiveness almost always helps motivate the people who phone volunteers to be enthusiastic in the rest of their contacts.

Some nonprofits keep information about their network volunteers in computer files available on printouts. Such files include names, addresses, telephone numbers, and brief summaries of information from past contacts with the volunteers. This information is especially helpful if a new staff person is phoning volunteers. You don't need a computer to keep the information (although a computer makes it easier). A simple list of volunteers, with basic information and space to keep handwritten summaries of contacts, is all that is essential.

6

Maximizing Your Impact with Coalitions

Major legislation is enacted most often through the combined efforts of a number of groups working in coalition, rather than through the efforts of a single organization. With rare exceptions, only a coalition can produce contacts varied and influential enough to achieve success on a major public policy issue.

At their best, coalitions coordinate and focus the resources of many groups that have a common interest in a legislative issue. A coalition may be formed for an effort that will take only several months, or the effort may take years. It depends on the significance of the changes sought. While coalitions have the potential to garner enormous legislative strength, they remain fragile. They are always subject to the danger that some members will become dissatisfied with the direction being taken and will unilaterally attempt to arrange a legislative compromise not supported by the majority. Despite that inherent weakness, the risk is worth taking to gain the strength that comes from a broad base.

Organizing a Coalition

There are a number of ways for you to determine whether there is interest among other groups in joining a coalition to work on a legislative issue. The simplest way is to describe, in a page or so, the problem as your organization sees it. Then invite groups to send representatives to a meeting. A person (perhaps yourself) whom all or most attendees know and respect should chair the first meeting. After several meetings, the group will probably want to select a permanent leader.

To avoid later misunderstandings, you should seek clear agreement from the outset on the goals of the coalition, how it will target its efforts, and how the undertaking will be financed. Financing is particularly important. If there is not clear agreement from the outset, the resulting dissension may undermine the coalition's effectiveness. As a coalition grows, a small "secretariat" is usually appointed. It is made up of the coalition's leaders and makes decisions that do not require the full coalition's approval.

The most important role of the secretariat is to build a sense of trust and openness, with honesty and "no surprises" paramount. Any compromises on legislation should be agreed to in advance by the coalition. The coalition may also give a small leadership group the power to make on-the-spot compromises. These are almost always required as legislation comes down to the finish line.

Every coalition must have one organization that serves as a clearinghouse. That organization attends, among other things, to all the exceedingly important mechanical details that go into the effective running of any meeting. (It is amazing how often such details, so important in making people feel at home, are neglected. A written agenda, name cards at each place, personal greetings by the host to each attendee, snacks—all these items help set the right tone for a meeting. Good attendance is aided if meetings are held at an established time and location and if coalition members are phoned in advance.) The clearinghouse organization also takes responsibility for receiving information from the coalition and, as necessary, passing that information on to coalition members, without delay. Because providing access to good, timely information is so important, the organization responsible for that function should be selected with great care.

Effective coalitions have leaders who recognize that the strength of the coalition, and therefore its ultimate success, rests with the coalition's members, not with its leaders. The leaders also recognize that their principal role is to serve the members by working hard at the unexciting but critically important details required for effective coordination with the clearinghouse organization.

Working with a Coalition

There will be an inclination on the part of some coalition members to think the job is done once the coalition gets started: "The coalition will do it." It is very important to get the message across early that the success or failure of the coalition depends on the action of all its members. Get members involved immediately. Give them specific tasks, and hold them accountable by asking them to report regularly at coalition meetings.

It is wise to assess in advance the strength of the commitment of those being asked to join the coalition. It is essential that at least some coalition members view the coalition's issue as also the top priority for their own organizations. If no one organization sees the issue as paramount among its

own concerns, it is almost impossible to generate the steam needed for a successful effort on a major legislative initiative. Passion will be lacking, and its absence always shows. The less passion there is, the more the coalition's effort will appear to legislators as simply another special-interest exercise, not as a reflection of constituents' real views. As a result, the coalition's effort will be largely discounted.

No coalition is ever fortunate enough to have its issue viewed as the top priority by the majority of its members. Moreover, the importance that individual coalition members assign to the issue often fluctuates during the life of the coalition, according to other legislative issues that the members may be addressing. Don't be disappointed if some members lose interest. That's in the nature of every coalition. Indeed, shifts in levels of enthusiasm provide a sense of renewal: Those who show increasing interest can be given additional responsibility, while others, for good reasons that may have nothing to do with the coalition's efforts or leaders, will fall by the wayside. But if, over time, you find that many of your members are losing interest, it will be important for you to contact the groups that have dropped out recently and determine whether their interest has waned because of some failure on the part of the coalition's leaders.

The lobbying techniques that coalitions use are essentially the same as those that individual organizations use. Coalition members, like all members of organizations, need accurate, brief, clear, timely information on which to take action. Timeliness is sometimes especially difficult in coalition activity because there may be as many as four steps in the process of getting information to people who are asked to take action. It goes from the coalition to the national organization and then to the state group and the local association, which sends the information to its members. To speed up the process when a key vote is coming up in the near future, it is important for a coalition to consider using the telephone, fax, and e-mail to get the word out quickly to its members. Nothing discourages a coalition member more than discovering that leaders were too late in getting them information on a crucial vote.

In making contacts with legislators, it is particularly helpful for coalition members to use the names of their individual organizations. Chances are that the legislator will be much more familiar with them than with the name of the coalition.

Legislation is one of the few areas of nonprofit organizational activity where there is a very clear outcome. Over time, you either succeed or fail in getting a measure enacted or voted down. Success in a legislative effort is almost like money in the bank for a nonprofit. If publicized appropriately, a legislative success is very helpful in attracting volunteers and funding, and so there is always a temptation for the coalition's organizational leaders to claim credit for the victory. But this is shortsighted, if not unfair. The more you give coalition members credit for a victory and make them feel that they had an important role, the more they will want to participate in the continuing battle (if it's not over) or participate in any new efforts that the coalition may want to make. Spread the credit around as widely as possible, and you will strengthen all the members of the coalition. Stifle the inclination to do otherwise or to go quickly on to other things. Forget to give public acclaim to each coalition member, and you will miss an opportunity.

7

Guidelines on Using a Government Relations Committee

The biggest mistake, bar none, made by government relations committees of nonprofits is to take on too many priorities. It is an understandable failing. In any nonprofit, so much needs to be done that volunteers as well as staff often cannot resist tackling yet another issue. As a result, the nonprofit often finds itself in the impossible situation of having several "number one" priority issues. Its efforts are spread so thin that nothing is done well.

A critically important rule that top volunteer and staff leaders must follow in any organization is to insist, painful though it may be, that the organization adopt only one top legislative priority. The committee can have 20 issues that it follows, but all must be ranked. There must be clear understanding that most of the issues will necessarily get only cursory attention.

Holding on to just one top priority is difficult. Committee members whose main interests are in different issues will push volunteers and staff people hard to give their issues top priority, even though the committee and the board have decided otherwise. Resist the temptation to give in. You may disappoint a key committee member, but you will serve your organization properly. Focusing on one issue at a time is the only way that you can marshal all your resources and ultimately prevail in the tough

environment you face in any legislative fight. While keeping to one priority is important, there should also be enough flexibility in your process for the committee to shift emphasis to the second or third priority, if it becomes very clear that little more can be achieved for the moment on the legislation that is the top priority.

How to Structure Your Government Relations Committee

A nonprofit's decisions on legislation are made by a variety of groups and individuals, but it is critically important to provide the means by which an established group has final authority to act when a legislative decision is needed immediately. That moment always comes, sooner or later, during the heat of a legislative campaign. When time doesn't permit consultation with the full government relations committee, two or three people should be given the authority to speak for the organization. That authority should be given on the basis of these people's judgment and their understanding of the positions already taken by the government relations committee, the board, and the full membership.

Because of the central role played by government relations activities in the overall programs of many nonprofits, most nonprofits give their committees policymaking rather than advisory status. Policymaking authority serves the useful function of permitting the committee to take positions and action on minor legislative issues without bringing them before the board. But be cautious. If the committee assumes too much authority, it may find itself without the power base to move a particular bill, because members may see the committee as having taken actions that the members did not really understand or support. Most nonprofits active in government relations give legislative activity a high priority. Therefore, it is important that the government relations committee, like the board of directors, be broadly representative of the organization's constituency.

Some committee members are valuable for their understanding of the legislative process; others, for their ability to chair subgroups of the committee; still others, for their contacts with influential members of the legislature. Some will be valuable because they understand the issues being addressed by the proposed legislation, even though they know little about the legislative process itself. The government relations committee sets the broad agenda, but much of the in-depth legislative work is delegated to task forces or other subgroups. These groups are usually headed by a member of the government relations committee.

Leading the Government Relations Committee

The most important attribute that the chair of your government relations committee can offer is his or her ability to lead. Expertise in the legislative process, although helpful, is not essential; other committee members and staff people have that knowledge. In nonprofits where government relations may be a key activity, it helps if the chair of the committee is a volunteer who both knows the organization well and has held key volunteer posts in the organization.

Being chair of the government relations committee gives the volunteer in that post very high visibility within the organization. Organizational leaders can provide that volunteer with an opportunity to strengthen his or her skills. Serving as chair of this key committee often proves to be a stepping-stone to higher positions in the organization.

Running the Committee Meeting

Nonprofits are noted for the number of meetings they hold. Strangely, however, their meetings are often not well conducted. There are ways to make a government relations committee meeting go smoothly. Staff members and the chair should meet well before the meeting, to determine what should be included in the meeting's agenda. Draw up an agenda packet, and include a cover note that states the main topics to be discussed. If the agenda packet also includes extensive readings, provide "executive summaries" (most committee members will not read lengthy materials). Mail the packet in time for members to receive it at least a week before the meeting. It also helps to provide brief biographical information on all committee members, including their addresses and telephone numbers. They may not know one another, and such a list will help them stay in touch.

At your last meeting of the year, set the meeting dates for the coming year. Send these dates to all committee members, and urge them to mark their calendars. A month before each meeting, send a reminder, along with an R.S.V.P. card. When in doubt, call several days before the meeting to confirm members' attendance.

Ask yourself what makes you feel at ease at a meeting. Greet each person at some point before the meeting begins. Provide extra agenda packets, and be certain to have a name card that stands upright (a "tent" card) at each person's place. (How often have you been embarrassed by having to hide the fact that you have forgotten the name of the person sitting across from you even though the two of you have met often in the past?) Unless you are very certain that everyone knows everyone else, have people introduce themselves. Go up to people who arrive late and greet them. Be certain that they have agenda packets and places at the table.

When more than one table is used, place the tables in a "square doughnut," so that all attendees will be facing the center and can all be heard easily. Check the room well before the meeting, to be certain that everything you have requested has been provided. Arrange for coffee and light snacks. You may be surprised how much they can help to set the right tone for your meeting.

This is sometimes very difficult, but don't let the chair, the staff, or any one person dominate the meeting. There is a strong temptation to stand aside when this happens. If you do, however, you stand to lose the interest, involvement, respect, and ultimately, the participation of the members. (For more information on these basic points, an excellent source is O'Connell, 1994; see especially the chapter called "Making the Most out of Meetings.")

8

Lobbying Through the Media

Legislators, because of the important role the media play in shaping public opinion, pay special attention to issues covered by the media in their legislative districts. They also take note of the organizations and individuals the media quote in news stories on those issues.

Congressional staff people rank both news articles and editorials in major daily newspapers very high as forces that influence members of Congress (Burson-Marsteller, 1992). Articles and editorials in smaller publications rank a bit lower but still high. Effective media relations can be an important means of getting a legislator's support and influencing public opinion on your legislative issue.

There are a number of techniques for getting your message into the media—press releases, calling a reporter or editor, press conferences, letters to the editor, press interviews—but none is a sure thing! You can never be sure that your publicity efforts will produce so much as one spoken or written word on behalf of your cause, but it is important to try. (Sample media ads and legislative alerts are included in Resource E.)

There are some media activities that your organization can conduct without in-depth understanding of media relations. For example, you can probably get some letters to a newspaper editor published by having key members of your

board, or others with influence in the community, write to the editor. If you plan to develop a media strategy and become involved in press conferences, press interviews, press releases, meetings with editorial boards, and so on, then you should either enlist the services of a volunteer with public relations experience or hire a professional. A person with experience in media relations can save your group an enormous amount of effort by helping you know how and where to target your efforts most effectively.

If you plan to hire a consultant or staff member to conduct media relations, nothing can be more important than making the right decision and knowing the person's track record firsthand. Get an assessment from someone whose judgment you greatly respect, someone specifically acquainted with the person's or the public relations firm's work. Don't depend entirely on the general reputation of the individual firm, and don't rely wholly on how it describes its services. The closest to a foolproof approach in hiring the right person is to take an individual from a public relations firm or a consultant group who has worked either with your organization or with someone whose opinion you trust.

In dealings with the media, send them information only if it is truly newsworthy. You will be quickly and permanently dismissed if your so-called news is unimportant, inaccurate, or untimely.

There is a herd instinct in the media. If one influential newspaper picks up your story, others may quickly follow suit and contact you. If you can be responsive to all, your issue may maintain momentum for several days or even longer. Equally important, if the media have come to you as a source on this issue, they will view you as a source on related issues.

Reporters look for quotable sources, people they can count on for good one- or two-sentence comments that will add color and credibility to a story. It is wise to have that supposedly off-the-cuff comment well rehearsed before you talk with the reporter. It is also essential to be well briefed on an issue before giving an interview.

There should be close coordination between your organization's lobbyist and its media coordinator. The lobbyist can help with the media by being available for comment on pending legislation. The media coordinator must keep abreast of fast-breaking action on the legislation, to know when and how to get information and comments to the media.

Keep a list of media people who have contacted you or have written or spoken on your issue. They will be an important resource for future press conferences and press releases.

Your organization can present information to the media in a number of ways that will draw more attention to your issue and increase the interest of the legislature. The following sections discuss several media techniques often used by nonprofit groups.

Press Releases

A press release can be used to make a statement or take a stand on actions by the legislature or the administration that affect your legislation. Whatever the subject of the press release, the information in it must be both important and new.

The release should be written concisely. The most important information should appear in the first paragraph, with the rest of the information given in descending order of importance. (Editors often cut paragraphs from the end of a story to fit it into the available space.)

The first page of a release should answer the "five w's"— *who, what, where, when,* and *why. You* will probably want to add *how* as well. Keep sentences and paragraphs brief. Use active rather than passive verbs, and hold the release to no more than a few pages. Accuracy in facts, spelling, and grammar are basic.

Type the release, double-spaced, on 8-1/2" x 11" paper, and use wide margins. At the top of the page, state the name of the individual or group releasing the information, the name of the person in the organization whom the press should contact for more information, and a telephone number to call for more information. Include release instructions: "For immediate release, January 1998" or "For release at 1 P.M., January 10, 1998." Use quotations where appropriate, and clearly identify your sources.

Press Conferences

It is usually difficult to get good attendance at press conferences, because there are always so many issues competing for the media's attention. If you are to have even moderate prospects for good attendance, your issue has to be particularly important and timely and your spokesperson well known.

Nothing can replace a skilled communications person in charge of making arrangements for a press conference. Whoever handles the conference should know the basics, including the hour of the day when reporters are most likely to attend, the location that will attract reporters, how far in advance the press must be notified and how best to do so, and which reporters are assigned to your issue. It is also important to give a reminder call on the day of the press conference. Have a well-written press statement and background materials available as handouts. Reporters often arrive, pick up those materials, and leave without waiting for the conference. Be certain that you have flawless audio equipment at the conference. Keep the press conference short, and leave time for a question-and-answer period. Always keep a list of those who have attended, for future follow-up.

Letters to the Editor

Letters to the editor can increase awareness of your issue. Sometimes letters are used to respond to negative editorials or press stories (although some experts say that responding to a negative editorial through a letter to the editor only reinforces the negative points by repeating them in order to refute them).

If you think your legislation will be enhanced by letters to the editor, there are several points to keep in mind. Your letter should be tightly composed and should use short sentences. Check with the newspaper to determine the length of letters it prints. Use strong, active verbs. Avoid adjectives. Use specific examples to make your points. Address only one point per letter. Use accurate, up-to-date information. Don't attack the opposition. Always sign your name, and include your address and telephone number.

Other Media Opportunities

Op-ed pieces, which appear opposite the newspaper's editorial page, provide an opportunity for individuals, well-known and not so well-known, to present in-depth views on various issues. Larger newspapers pay modest sums for op-ed pieces and assign editorial people to their op-ed pages.

Editorial boards of newspapers sometimes meet with spokespersons from organizations that want to present their points of view on issues. With small and medium-sized newspapers, it is helpful to submit draft editorials. Small newspapers may print them word for word; bigger editorial staffs may find them useful in composing their own editorials. It's very important to thank reporters for their stories about your issue and to provide them with important new information that may constitute material for follow-up stories. Keep a file of reporters who have written on your issue.

Special Opportunities with Radio and Television

Radio and television offer several kinds of opportunities for getting your message across. Some are specific to each medium and others are common to both. Radio and TV stations are accessible. Topics for talk shows, editorial themes, news stories—stations need all of these daily. Maybe you can help them fill their time and your needs.

The most obvious method is to get your story to the news departments of local radio and television stations. When circulating a news release to the print media, don't forget the news directors of radio and television stations. Most stations do have less time for news than newspapers have space, and so there is keen competition for stories, but keep trying. If you have a news-only station in your community, definitely go for it.

In the case of television news, it will help greatly if there is a visual angle to the story. If you can center the story on an interesting visual location, your chances are much better for making the TV news. Likewise, you may also want to consider a good visual location for a news conference—keeping in mind, of course, that news conferences should not be held unless you have real news to announce.

You can produce public service announcements for both radio and television, although some television spots are very expensive. Radio and television stations do offer public service time on a regular basis. The Federal Communications Commission no longer requires them to offer a specific amount of time, but most continue to provide some, to show that they are community-minded.

Your best chance of having both your radio and your TV public service spots used is to keep them short—about ten seconds for TV, and preferably nine. Perhaps you can supply one or two color slides to go with them. A television station may assist you in producing a video spot. It happens occasionally. It doesn't hurt to ask. But please understand if the station is too busy to do it.

Radio public service announcements can be longer—perhaps 20 or 30 seconds. Sometimes, however, just a sentence or two, targeted for use by a popular disc jockey several times during the day, can be very effective.

You can try to get your spokesperson on a radio or TV talk show. Perhaps your spokesperson can appear on a local call-in show. In either case, particularly the latter, be sure that the spokesperson is fully briefed on the issue and is prepared for criticism and strong comments from the opposite point of view.

You should not forget radio and television editorials. "What do you mean?" you may ask. "Radio and TV station managers write those, don't they?" Yes, they do. Most people don't realize, however, that many of those editorials are inspired and influenced by outside individuals and groups. Just as news tips come from outside in many cases, so do ideas for editorials. Again, it's not a sure thing, by any means. Station managers have to determine whether an issue is important to them and whether they agree with your side of the issue. But you can get in, and that chance is worth the effort to try.

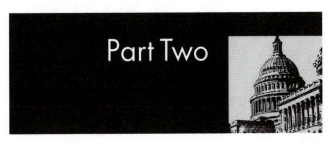

Part Two

A Guide to
**Technical
Issues** Related to
Lobbying by
**501(c)(3)
Organizations**

The intent of Part Two is to provide enough information to volunteers and staff, especially to those who are new to lobbying, so that they will have a beginning understanding of it. This material should not replace legal counsel. If you have questions regarding any of the technical information, it will be important for you to consult with an attorney. Just remember that in the author's opinion, attorneys, with some notable exceptions, tend to be too cautious about encouraging nonprofits to lobby.

This book is about lobbying by nonprofits that are tax exempt under Section 501(c)(3) of the Internal Revenue Code. There are some limitations on the amount of lobbying a 501(c)(3) may conduct and those limitations are outlined in Chapter 9.

One important difference between 501(c)(3) organizations and 501(c)(4)s is that charitable contributions are tax deductible to the former, but not to the latter. Additional information on lobbying by 501(c)(4) groups is provided in Chapter 10.

9

The 1976 Lobby Law and 1990 IRS Regulations: An Overview

In 1976, Congress passed landmark legislation that clarified and greatly expanded the extent to which nonprofits could lobby without jeopardizing their tax-exempt status. That legislation, Section 1307 of Public Law 94-455, recognized lobbying as an entirely proper function of nonprofits and ended the uncertainty about lobbying by groups that are tax-exempt under Section 501(c)(3) of the Internal Revenue Code.[2]

It took a full 14 years for the Internal Revenue Service to issue final regulations under the 1976 lobby law, but the regulations were worth the wait. While the last four years included some stormy debate between nonprofits and the IRS regarding earlier proposed regulations, the final version, issued on August 31, 1990, is faithful to the 1976 law, which greatly extended the lobbying rights of nonprofits. There is clear consensus in the nonprofit community that the regulations provide a framework that will prove to be both flexible and workable for nonprofits' efforts on legislation. In every critical area, the regulations reflect responsiveness to (although not complete acceptance of) the criticisms and suggestions offered by nonprofits during the long process that led to the final outcome.

In understanding the 1976 lobby law, it helps to know that lobbying, for a nonprofit electing to come under the law, is only the expenditure of money by the organization for the purpose of attempting to influence legislation. Where there is no expenditure by the organization for lobbying, there is no lobbying by the organization. Therefore, lobbying by a volunteer for a nonprofit is not counted as a lobbying expenditure to the organization and is *not* lobbying. If, however, the volunteer is reimbursed by the nonprofit for out-of-pocket expenditures, then the reimbursed funds do count as a lobbying expenditure. But it's important to keep in mind the point that *lobbying occurs only when there is an expenditure of funds* for an activity that meets the other criteria for lobbying.

It is also helpful in understanding the 1976 law to recognize that the law defines two kinds of lobbying: direct lobbying and grassroots lobbying. To oversimplify, the term *direct lobbying* means communications that your organization has about legislation (1) with legislators or government officials who participate in the formulation of legislation and (2) with its own members. Direct lobbying would include visiting a congressperson about a bill and being in touch with your organization's members and urging them to contact legislators. The term *grassroots lobbying* refers to any attempt to influence legislation through an attempt to affect the opinion of the general public. The ceiling for a nonprofit's spending on grassroots lobbying is one-fourth of the total allowable lobbying expenditures.

Sometimes groups confuse urging their members to lobby with grassroots lobbying of the general public. They

---

[2] Public Law 94-455 resulted in Internal Revenue Code Sections 4911 and 501(h). Section 4911 includes information on how much can be spent on lobbying. Section 501(h) provides information on electing to come under the provisions of PL 94-455.

mistakenly think that contacting their members, who may number hundreds of thousands, to urge them in turn to contact members of the legislature constitutes grassroots lobbying, simply because those members are at the grassroots level. Only when an organization is trying to reach beyond its members to get action from the general public does grassroots lobbying occur.

The following information on the 1976 law is fairly detailed, but don't be discouraged by all the detail. Keep in mind that the provisions of the law are very liberal. They provide all the lobbying latitude that 99 out of 100 groups will ever need. The details included here will help provide the assurance you may need that many of your activities in the legislative arena are not lobbying under the 1976 lobby law.

Virtually all of the information that follows in this chapter is drawn from materials written for INDEPENDENT SECTOR by Walter B. Slocombe formerly of Caplin & Drysdale, Washington, D.C. It is an overview of the lobbying latitude permitted to 501(c)(3) organizations under the 1976 law and regulations.

Nonprofit Lobbying: An Overview

What Groups Are Affected?

The regulations are effective for an organization's first tax year that begins after their publication, which took place on August 31, 1990. Nonprofits that have elected to come under the 1976 lobby law need to familiarize themselves with the regulations, so that they will know what activities will and will not count against the statutory limits, and so that they can correctly calculate the amounts they treat as spending for lobbying.

Private foundations are affected. This is because the regulations (1) elaborate the standards that foundations must meet to comply with the general ban on lobbying by private foundations and (2) establish guidelines for grants by private foundations to nonprofits that elect to come under the law.

Nonprofits that have any degree of involvement in public policy issues also have an interest in the regulations, even if they have not elected to be covered by them. This interest arises partly because nonprofits need to decide whether to make that election, and partly because, although the regulations nominally apply to nonprofits only if they have so elected, the standards set forth in the regulations may affect the application of the old "substantiality" standard, to which nonelecting nonprofits will remain subject.

How Does the Tax Law Regulate Public Charities' Lobbying?

The general rule of Section 501(c)(3), to which all organizations exempt under that provision are subject unless they elect to come under the 1976 lobby law, is that "no substantial part" of their activities may be that of attempting to influence legislation. Although the provision has been in the IRS code since 1934 and has occasionally been applied by the courts, there has never been a clear definition of the point at which lobbying becomes substantial or, indeed, of what activities related to public policy and to controversial subjects constitute attempts to influence legislation. In particular, the IRS position is that spending, as a share of budget, is far from the sole measure of whether a nonelecting group's lobbying is substantial; such factors as absolute amount spent, impact, public prominence, and unpaid volunteer work also enter into the determination.

To clarify and liberalize the rules for lobbying by nonprofits, Section 501(h) and 4911 were added to the code in 1976, as a result of the enactment of the 1976 lobby law. In outline, the provisions permit most nonprofits (but not churches, their integrated auxiliaries, or a convention or association of churches) to elect to have their legislative efforts governed by the specific rules of Sections 501(h) and 4911, instead of the vague "substantiality" standard. To that end, the 1976 legislation both sets financial limits for lobbying activities and defines the activities that count against those limits.

What Are the Main Elements of the 1976 Law?

—Exclusions from Lobbying.

Critical to the 1976 law are the provisions declaring that many expenditures that have some relationship to public policy and legislative issues are not treated as lobbying and so are permitted without limit. For example:

1. Contacts with executive branch employees or legislators in support of or opposition to proposed regulations is not considered lobbying. So, if your nonprofit is trying to get a regulation changed it may contact both members of the executive branch as well as legislators to urge support for your position on the regulation and the action is not considered lobbying.
2. Lobbying by volunteers is considered a lobbying expenditure only to the extent that the nonprofit incurs expenses associated with the volunteers' lobbying. For example, volunteers working for a nonprofit could organize a huge rally of volunteers at the state capitol to lobby on an issue and the only expenses related to the rally paid by the nonprofit would count as a lobbying expenditure.
3. A nonprofit's communications to its members on legislation—even if it takes a position on the legislation—is not lobbying so long as the nonprofit doesn't directly encourage its members or others to lobby. For example, a group could send out a public affairs bulletin to its members, take a position on legislation in the bulletin, and it would not count as lobbying if the nonprofit didn't ask its members to take action on the measure.
4. A nonprofit's response to written requests from a legislative body (not just a single legislator) for technical advice on pending legislation is not considered lobbying. So, if requested in writing a group could provide testimony on legislation, take a position in the testimony on that legislation, and it would not be considered lobbying.
5. So-called self-defense activity—that is, lobbying legislators (but not the general public) on matters that may affect the organization's own existence, powers, tax exempt status, and similar matters would not be lobbying. For example, lobbying in opposition to proposals in Congress to curtail nonprofit lobbying, or lobbying in support of a charitable tax deduction for nonitemizers,

would not be a lobbying expenditure. It would become lobbying only if you asked for support from the general public.

[Lobbying for programs in the organization's field, (e.g., health, welfare, environment, education, etc.) however, is not self-defense lobbying. For example, an organization that is fighting to cure cancer could not consider working for increased appropriations for cancer research to be self-defense lobbying.]

6. Making available the results of "nonpartisan analysis, study, or research" on a legislative issue that presents a sufficiently full and fair exposition of the pertinent facts to enable the audience to form an independent opinion, would not be considered lobbying. The regulations make clear that such research and analysis need not be "neutral" or "objective" to fall within this "nonpartisan" exclusion. The exclusion is available to research and analysis that take direct positions on the merits of legislation, as long as the organization presents facts fully and fairly, makes the material generally available, and does not include a direct call to the reader to contact legislators. This exception is particularly important because many nonprofits that engage in public policy do conduct significant amounts of nonpartisan analysis, study, and research on legislation.

7. A nonprofit's discussion of broad social, economic, and similar policy issues whose resolution would require legislation—even if specific legislation on the matter is pending—is not considered lobbying so long as the discussion does not address the merits of specific legislation. For example, a session at a nonprofit's annual meeting regarding the importance of enacting child welfare legislation, would not be lobbying so long as the organization is not addressing merits of specific child welfare legislation pending in the legislature. Representatives of the organizations would even talk directly to legislators on the broad issue of child welfare, so long as there is no reference to specific legislation on that issue.

8. It's not grassroots lobbying if a nonprofit urges the public, through the media or other means, to vote for or against a ballot initiative or referendum. (It's direct lobbying, not grassroots, because the public in this situation becomes the legislature. Lobbying the public through the media is therefore considered a direct lobbying expenditure, not a grassroots expenditure. This is an advantage because nonprofits are permitted to spend more on direct lobbying than on grassroots lobbying.)

From the foregoing, it is very clear that there are many activities related to legislation that do not count toward lobbying expenditure limits.

—Permitted Levels of Spending for Lobbying. The second key element of the 1976 law is that it unequivocally declares that activities that do constitute active lobbying are permitted, provided only that they fall within the spending ceilings established by the law. The spending ceilings are based on percentages of the nonprofit's budget for the year, beginning at 20 percent of the first $500,000 and ending at 5 percent of expenditures over $1.5 million. (Strictly speaking, the base is the nonprofit's exempt-purpose expenditures, which include all payments for the organization's programs and exempt purposes but exclude costs of investment management, unrelated businesses, and certain fund-raising costs.) There is an overall maximum ceiling of $1 million a year. The effect of the sliding-scale ceilings is that an organization reaches the maximum permissible ceiling when its exempt-purpose expenditures reach $17 million.

Expenditures for grassroots lobbying—that is, attempting "to influence legislation through an attempt to affect the opinions of the general public or any segment thereof"—are limited to one-quarter of the overall ceiling, as already stated. Amounts spent on lobbying in excess of that level must be for direct lobbying—that is, for communications made directly to legislators and their staffs and to executive-branch officials who participate in the formulation of legislation. (As previously described, communications with an organization's members that urge them to contact legislators are also treated as direct, rather than grassroots, lobbying. The total and grassroots ceilings at various exempt-purpose expenditure levels are shown in Table 3.) Since the amount that may be spent on grassroots lobbying is limited to one-quarter of the overall lobbying limit, if an organization's total lobbying limit is $100,000, then it may spend the full $100,000 on direct lobbying or it may spend up to $25,000 on grassroots lobbying and the rest on direct lobbying. Even if it chooses to spend nothing on direct lobbying, it will still be limited to $125,000 on grassroots lobbying.

Table 3. Lobbying Ceilings under the 1976 Lobby Law

Exempt-Purpose Expenditures	Total Lobbying Expenditures	Amount of Total Allowable for Grassroots Lobbying
Up to $500,000	20% of exempt-purpose expenditures	One-quarter
$500,000–$1 million	$100,000 + 15% of excess over $500,000	$25,000 + 3.75% of excess over $500,000
$1 million–$1.5 million	$175,000 + 10% of excess over $1 million	$43,750 + 2.5% of excess over $1 million
$1.5 million–$17 million	$225,000 + 5% of excess over $1.5 million	$56,250 + 1.25% of excess over $1.5 million
Over $17 million	$1 million	$250,000

—Flexible Sanctions. A third important element of the 1976 legislation was the establishment of a new and more flexible system of sanctions, to replace the "death sentence" of loss of exemption as the principal sanction for violation of the "substantiality" standard. (Since 1976, Congress has added additional sanctions, beyond loss of exemption, for non-electing organizations that violate that standard—a 5 percent excise tax on excessive lobbying spending, and a similar tax on managers who willfully and unreasonably agree to lobbying expenditures, knowing that these are likely to cause loss of exemption.) The initial sanction for nonprofits under the 1976 law that spend more than either the overall or the grassroots limit is a 25 percent excise tax on the lobbying spending in any year in excess of the ceiling. (If both ceilings are exceeded, the tax is on the greater of the two excess amounts.) Loss of exemption is an available sanction only if spending normally exceeds 150 percent of either the overall or the grassroots limit, generally determined by aggregating both spending and limits over a four-year period.

What Spending Counts Against the Limits?

There is considerable uncertainty about what activity counts against the "substantiality" standard, but the standard, under the 1976 lobby law, is strictly financial. The only factor that must be taken into account is the cost of communications for direct or grassroots lobbying, including the cost of preparing the communication (such as staff time, facilities, and allocable overhead).

—Elements Required for a Lobbying Communication. To be a direct lobbying communication, and therefore to count against the direct lobbying limits, a communication must refer to specific legislation and reflect a point of view on its merits. "Specific legislation" includes a specific measure that has not yet been introduced but does not include general concepts for solving problems that have not yet been reduced to legislative proposals.

To be a grassroots lobbying communication, subject to the lower ceiling, in most cases, a communication must, apart from referring to specific legislation and reflecting a view on it, encourage recipients to contact legislators. Under the regulations, such a call to action exists only when the material directly tells its audience to contact legislators; provides a legislator's address, phone number, or similar information; provides a petition, postcard, or other prepared message to be sent to the legislator; or identifies one or more legislators as opposing the organization's views, being undecided, being recipients' representative(s), or being a member of the committee that will consider the legislation.

Under these rules, a nonprofit (except in the narrow case of "highly publicized legislation," to be discussed) can make any public statement it likes about a legislative issue, without having the costs counted against its grassroots lobbying limit—as long as it avoids calls to action. The broad freedom that this rule gives nonprofits to discuss issues freely, as long as they forego calls to action, is shown by an example in the regulations. It concerns a mass-media advertisement that the IRS says would not normally be considered grassroots lobbying, because it lacks such a call. The sample advertisement reads as follows: "The State Assembly is considering a bill to make gun ownership illegal. This outrageous legislation would violate your constitutional rights and the rights of other law abiding citizens. If this legislation is passed, you and your family will be criminals if you want to exercise your right to protect yourselves."

—Special Rule for Paid Mass-Media Messages Close to Votes on "Famous" Bills. There is one exception to the rule stating that a public communication about legislation must include a call to action in order to be considered lobbying. The regulations eliminate the "call to action" requirement in a narrowly defined set of cases involving mass-media advertising just before a vote on certain legislation that has elicited a high degree of public awareness. These regulations apply—and communications can be considered grassroots lobbying, even without a call to the public to communicate with legislators about the legislation—only when all the following conditions are met:

1. The legislation in question has received so much publicity that its pendency or its general terms, purpose, or effect are known to a significant element of the general public, not just to the particular interest groups directly affected. The degree of publicity given the legislation is a factor here, but there must not only be publicity; there must also be general public knowledge about the particular legislation.

2. The nonprofit has bought paid advertising in the mass media (meaning television, radio, billboards, or general-circulation newspapers and magazines). Direct mail and the organization's own media outlets are not considered paid media, except for radio and television broadcasting by the organization itself and organization-published periodicals that have a circulation of 100,000, more than half of which is outside the organization's membership.

3. The advertising appears within two weeks before a vote will be taken in a full house or full committee (not just a subcommittee).

4. The advertisement either
   a. refers directly to the legislation (as in the gun control ad above) but does not include a call to action, as defined under the general standards,[3] or
   b. states a view on the general subject of the legislation and urges the public to communicate with legislators about that subject. (To carry on the handgun example, such an ad might say, "Let your state assemblyman know you want to protect your right to keep and bear arms"—without referring directly to the pending bill.)

Even when all these conditions are present, the organization can avoid counting the ad as a lobbying cost if it can show that it has customarily run such ads without regard to the timing of legislation, or that the particular ad's timing was unrelated to the upcoming

[3] If the ad includes a call to action, it is grassroots lobbying without the special "mass media" rules.

legislative action (as may be the case when television ads are bought under conditions that allow the station to determine when they run). This special rule for ads on highly publicized and well-known legislation affect few if any activities that are not directly and consciously aimed at legislative results. Even in those cases, of course, the activity is permitted within financial ceilings.

—Special Rule for Referenda, Initiatives, and Similar Procedures. In general, legislative messages aimed at the public as a whole are grassroots lobbying if they meet the "call to action" standard. The final regulations, however, recognize that in the case of referenda, initiatives, and similar procedures, the public is itself the legislature. Accordingly, communications to the public that refer to such measures and that take a stand on them are treated as direct lobbying of a legislature—subject only to the higher ceiling. The effect of these rules is that communications (newspaper ads, for example) that refer to a ballot measure and reflect a view on it are direct lobbying, whether or not they explicitly tell people how to vote.

This rule gives nonprofits important flexibility to be active in referendum efforts, which would have been impractical if they had been forced to count against the lower grassroots lobbying limits.

When Does Later Use of Materials in Lobbying Cause Their Costs to Be Counted as Lobbying?

The costs of a lobbying communication include the costs of the staff and facilities needed to prepare it, not just the costs of paper and ink or videotape. An issue of concern to many groups, especially those doing research on public policy issues, has been the possibility that research costs might be treated as costs of preparing to lobby, if the published results of the research were later referred to and used in lobbying. The final regulations on this so-called "subsequent use" issue should greatly ease organizations' concerns that their lobbying spending will be boosted unexpectedly because materials they have prepared are later used in lobbying— whether the use is by the organization itself, by a related organization, or by a third party. This is because costs of materials that are not themselves used for lobbying need to be counted as lobbying-support costs (on the basis of their later use in lobbying) *only* in cases in which all of the following conditions exist:

1. The materials both refer to and reflect a view on specific legislation. (They do not, however, in their initial format, include a call to action. If the materials do include such a call, their public circulation would itself be grassroots lobbying.) Materials— such as raw research data—that do not meet this test are entirely outside the "subsequent use" rules.
2. The lobbying use occurs within six months of payment for the materials. Therefore, lobbying use more than six months after a research project is complete cannot affect the

organization's lobbying costs. In any case, only the most recent six months of spending potentially represents a lobbying cost. There is no risk that, because of some lobbying use of research results more than six months after a project is finished, years of accumulated research spending will be treated as lobbying costs.

3. The organization fails to make a substantial nonlobbying distribution of the materials before the lobbying use. If the materials are "nonpartisan, analysis, study, or research," a nonlobbying distribution qualifies as "substantial" (and therefore excludes all the costs from lobbying treatment) if it conforms to the normal distribution pattern for similar materials, as followed by that organization and similar ones. For other materials, the nonlobbying distribution must be at least as extensive as the lobbying distribution. This rule means that, by seeing that research-and-analysis materials that take positions on legislation are first distributed to the public in normal ways, an organization can prevent their costs from being treated as lobbying costs, even if the materials are later used in lobbying by the organization itself or by an affiliate.

4. The organization's primary purpose in creating the materials was to use them in lobbying rather than for some nonlobbying goal. When the lobbying use is by an unrelated organization, not only must there be

clear and convincing evidence of such a lobbying purpose but that evidence must also include evidence of collusion and cooperation with the organization using the material for lobbying.

For private foundations making grants to nonprofits that spend the money on materials later used in lobbying, there is another layer of protection. Even if the grantee violates the "subsequent use" rules, the grantor foundation can be taxed on the grant as a lobbying expenditure only if the private foundation had a primary lobbying purpose in making the grant or if the grantmaking foundation knew or should reasonably have known of the grantee's lobbying purpose.

The cumulative effect of these safeguards is that a research organization can readily avoid any risk of unexpected lobbying expenses. Only costs that are less than six months old can be at issue. Even in theory, the problem can arise only in the case of material that takes a position on specific legislation. Even for such materials, there is a safe harbor for distributions that follow the normal patterns of dissemination. In any event, an organization can avoid having costs for materials later used in lobbying treated as grassroots lobbying cost if the primary purpose of incurring the cost was a nonlobbying objective. If the later use is by an unrelated organization, there must be clear and convincing evidence that the organization developed the research for the purpose of lobbying.

Does Electing to Be Governed by the New Regulations Complicate Receiving Grants from Foundations?

Private foundations may not elect to come under the 1976 law, and they remain absolutely prohibited from making expenditures for lobbying purposes. Therefore, some foundations have been concerned about their ability to make grants to nonprofits that explicitly adopt programs of lobbying by electing to come under the 1976 lobby law, and some nonprofits have worried that making an election under the 1976 law will scare off foundation funders.

The regulations—codifying and even liberalizing long-established IRS policy—meet these concerns by setting up a highly protective system for grants by private foundations to nonprofits that elect to come under the 1976 law. Under these rules, a foundation may make without tax liability a general-purpose grant to a nonprofit that lobbies, whether or not the nonprofit has elected. A private foundation may also make a grant to support a specific project that includes lobbying, as long as its own grant is less than the amount budgeted for the nonlobbying parts of the project. For example, if a specific project has a $200,000 budget, of which $20,000 is to be spent for lobbying, a private foundation can give the project up to $180,000 because that is the part of the project budget allocated to nonlobbying uses. The fact that other private foundations have already made grants for the project need not be taken into account in considering how much a private foundation can give. Of course, the foundation cannot earmark its funds for lobbying, nor can a foundation

support research in a case where the foundation itself has a primary lobbying purpose and where the results are used in violation of the "subsequent use" rules.

The regulations make clear that a foundation can rely on statements by the prospective grantee regarding how much the project will spend on lobbying, unless the foundation knows or has reason to know that the statements are false. The regulations also make clear that as long as the granting foundation complies with these standards when it makes the grant, it will not be held to have made a taxable lobbying expenditure if the nonprofit violates the assurances it gave when seeking the grant.

When Will a Nonprofit's Transfers to a Lobbying Organization Be Counted as Lobbying Expenditures?

If a nonprofit pays another organization or an individual to do lobbying for it, the payment counts against its direct or grassroots lobbying ceiling according to the character of the work done. The regulations also seek to prevent evasion of the limits by nonprofits that provide funds to other organizations not subject to the Section 501(c)(3) lobbying limits—such as presumably a related organization exempt under Section 501(c)(4)—to increase the resources available for the recipient's lobbying efforts. In such a case, the funds transferred are deemed to have been paid for grassroots lobbying, to the extent of the transferee's grassroots lobbying expenditures, with any remaining amount treated as having been paid for direct lobbying, to the extent of the transferee's direct lobbying expenditures.

This rule is subject to some very important qualifications, however. There is no lobbying expenditure when a nonprofit makes a grant to a nonprofit and the grant's use is expressly limited to a specific educational or otherwise nonprofit purpose and when records demonstrate that use. The regulations also make clear that the rule does not apply when the nonprofit is getting fair market value for the money it transfers. Thus, if a 501(c)(3) organization pays rent at fair market value to a 501(c)(4) group, or if the 501(c)(3) group pays to a 501(c)(4) group its proper portion of the costs of a shared employee, the rule does not apply, because the 501(c)(3) group is getting full value from the 501(c)(4) group.

These transfer rules protect nonprofits that engage in normal and legitimate transactions with related (or unrelated) entities. Such nonprofits need only follow the substantive and accounting procedures that are required in any case for general tax purposes, without regard to the special lobbying provisions.

How Are Expenditures That Have Both Lobbying and Nonlobbying Purposes Treated?

Sometimes a nonprofit wants to distribute a communication that has both lobbying and nonlobbying messages, such as a mass mailing that calls for readers to contact legislators about pending legislation and also asks them for contributions to the organization. In general, the regulations permit allocation between the lobbying and nonlobbying aspects of such mixed-purpose communications; but, to reflect the special solicitude that is extended to communications with members,

treatment of such communications is more generous.

The details are beyond the scope of this overview, but the general situation is as follows. First, costs of communications with members may be allocated, as between lobbying and any other bona fide nonlobbying purpose (education, fund raising, or advocacy on nonlegislative issues), on any reasonable basis. An attempt to allocate to lobbying only the particular words actually urging legislative action—and not the material explaining the legislative issue and the organization's position—will be rejected as unreasonable. Second, costs for part-lobbying communications to nonmembers (including even the membership share, if the communications go primarily to nonmembers) can be allocated to nonlobbying purposes only to the extent they do not address the "same specific subject" as the legislative message in the communication. The same specific subject is rather broadly defined to include activities that would be affected by legislation addressed elsewhere in the message, as well as the background and consequences of the legislation and activities affected by it. Nevertheless, fund raising and providing general information about the organization are not treated as being on the same specific subject as a legislative message. Therefore, that share of costs attributable to those goals would not be a lobbying expenditure. Allocation of costs away from lobbying is also permitted for the parts of a communication that are discussions of distinct aspects of a broad problem, one feature of which would be affected by the legislation addressed elsewhere in the communication.

Organizations that have extensive and expensive direct-mail operations aimed at current contributors (who are members) and prospects (who are not) will need to review their mailings, to ensure that they do not inadvertently make large grassroots lobbying expenditures. Similarly, groups that routinely send legislative alerts to nonmembers may want to make them distinct publications, rather than combining them with general communications.

When Are Several Nonprofits Treated on an Aggregate Basis?

In general, ceiling determinations and lobbying expenditure calculations are made on a separate basis for each legally distinct 501(c)(3) organization. Only if two or more organizations are subject to common control through interlocking majorities on their boards (or to common control by a third organization), or if one organization is required by its governing instrument to follow the legislative decisions of another, are the organizations aggregated under a single ceiling, with aggregate computations of expenditures. The requirement to follow legislative decisions must be express and not merely implied.

For Further Information

The preceding analysis is intended to give interested volunteers and staff members an overview, in lay language, of the 1976 lobby law. No guide, however, can adequately substitute for official information. Those wishing to make their own analyses will find the following additional sources to be of value:

- U.S. Internal Revenue Code of 1986, as amended, especially Sections 501(a), 501(c)(3), 501(h), and 4911.

- Public Law no. 94-455, The Tax Reform Act of 1976, approved October 4, 1976 (specifically, Section 1307, "Lobbying by Public Charities").
- House Report no. 94-1210, "Influencing Legislation by Public Charities," June 2, 1976, to accompany H.R. 13500. (H.R. 13500 became Section 1307 of PL 94-455.)
- Senate Report no. 94-938, Part 2, supplemental report on additional amendment to H.R. 10612, July 20, 1976. (H.R. 10612 became PL 94-455.)
- House Report no. 94-1515, conference report on H.R. 10612, September 13, 1976.
- "Final Regulations on Lobbying by Public Charities and Private Foundations." *Federal Register*, Aug. 31, 1990, p. 35579.

Election Procedure for Nonprofits

The process for electing to come under the 1976 lobby law (PL 94-455) is very simple. Those eligible to so elect are nonprofits exempt from taxation by Section 501(c)(3) of the Internal Revenue Code. The legislation does not apply to churches, their integrated auxiliaries, or a convention or association of churches. Private foundations also are not eligible, although they may make grants to nonprofits that do elect.

If a nonprofit does not elect to take advantage of the generous lobbying provisions under the 1976 lobby law, it remains subject to the vague "insubstantial" rule that has been in the tax code since 1934. Under that provision, if a nonprofit engages in more than insubstantial lobbying, it loses its Section 501(c)(3) status and its right to receive tax-deductible charitable contributions. Unfortunately, insubstantial has never been defined under the law, with the result that nonprofits that do lobby but have not elected to come under the 1976 law cannot be certain how much lobbying they may conduct without jeopardizing their tax-exempt status. Many nonprofits have followed the questionable guideline that the expenditure of 5 percent of their total annual expenditures on lobbying is not substantial and is therefore within the law. They have assumed that 5 percent of their *expenditures* is permissible because of a 1955 Sixth Circuit Court of Appeals ruling to the effect that attempts to influence legislation that constitute 5 percent of total *activities* are not substantial.

There is good reason to doubt that the "5 percent test" should be relied on. It was called into question by a 1972 ruling, which rejected a percentage test in determining what constituted substantial lobbying. In that case, the Tenth Circuit Court of Appeals supported a "facts and circumstances" test instead of a percentage test. In a 1974 ruling, the Claims Court stated that a percentage test was deemed inappropriate for determining whether lobbying activities are substantial. It was found that an exempt organization enjoying considerable prestige and influence could be considered as having a substantial impact on the legislative process, solely on the basis of making a single official position statement—an activity that would be considered negligible if measured according to a percentage standard of time expended. It is clearly in the interest of every nonprofit that lobbies more than a nominal amount to consider electing to come under the provisions of the 1976 law.

The law makes the process for electing very easy. A nonprofit's governing body—that is, its executive committee, board of directors, other representatives, or total membership, according to the constitution or bylaws of the particular nonprofit—may elect to have the organization come under the law. An authorized officer or trustee signs the one-page Internal Revenue Service Form 5768 and checks the box marked "Election." (A copy of IRS Form 5768 is in Resource E.) Regardless of the actual date of election, the nonprofit is considered to have come under the provisions of the law as of the start of the tax year during which it files the election.

The nonprofit automatically continues under the provisions of the 1976 law unless it chooses to revoke that election. It can do that by having its governing body vote on revocation and having an authorized officer or trustee sign another Form 5768. The revocation becomes effective at the start of the tax year that follows the date of the revocation. In other words, revocation can only be prospective.

A new nonprofit may elect to come under the lobby law even before it is determined to be eligible by the IRS. It simply submits Form 5768 at the time it submits its "Application for Recognition of Exemption" (Form 1023). Offices and addresses for obtaining IRS Form 5768 are listed in Resource F. The nonprofit's employer identification number, which is requested at the top of the form, is listed on the nonprofit's "Employer Quarterly Federal Tax Return" (Form 941).

One final important note: Some nonprofits have been reluctant to come under the 1976 lobby law, for fear that taking this action will serve as a "red flag" to the IRS and prompt an audit of lobbying activities. Fortunately, this is not the case. The IRS, in an October 7, 1988, letter to attorneys representing INDEPENDENT SECTOR, made clear that it does not plan to single out nonprofit organizations that elect to come under the provisions of the 1976 law. (Earlier, the IRS had furnished each IRS region with a listing of organizations that had elected to come under the 1976 law, and that action had raised fears among some nonprofits that the IRS planned to target for audit the lobbying activities of those nonprofits that had elected.) In the letter, the IRS representative said,

> As I stated above, our intent has been, and continues to be, one of encouragement [of nonprofit organizations] to make the election. Accordingly, I am taking steps to see that the IR Manual provision on this is revised. I have instructed that the IR Manual clarify that the filing of an election is a neutral factor for audit selection purposes. This change should eliminate the perception and concerns expressed in your letter."

In compliance with that promise, the Internal Revenue Manual now states, "Experience also suggests that organizations that have made the election [under the 1976 lobby law] are usually in compliance with the restrictions on legislative activities, so they do not appear to justify an effort to examine solely on this issue."

When Congress was debating the 1976 lobby law, before its enactment, there was clear evidence that Congress fully intended the law to encourage nonprofits to lobby and not to discourage them by singling them out for audit. These facts should reassure nonprofit groups that they will not be targeted for lobbying audits if they elect to be covered under the 1976 law.

10

Special Issues and Regulations

Lobbying by Nonprofits on Initiatives and Referenda

An initiative is a procedure by which a specified number of voters propose a statute, constitutional amendment, or ordinance and compel a popular vote on its adoption. One good example of nonprofits' effective use of the initiative process to achieve their program goals is the continuing successful efforts of state and local affiliates of the American Cancer Society, the American Heart Association, and the American Lung Association. Working in coalition, they have had the banning of smoking in public facilities put to a vote in a number of states and communities.

Sometimes called "do-it-yourself government" because they bypass legislative bodies, initiatives cover a wide variety of issues: a nuclear-arms freeze, tax cuts, reduced state spending, deposits on soft-drink bottles, civilians' use of nuclear power to generate electricity, greater citizen control over state supervision or regulation of electric utilities, prohibitions on abortion funding for low-income women, changing the way state or local legislatures are redistricted, rules related to payroll deduction of union dues used for political purposes and changes in state laws dealing with crime. The initiative involves getting the number of signatures

of bona fide voters required by the state constitution or local charter to sign petitions mandating the legislature to place the issue on the ballot. It is expensive and cumbersome to get an initiative all the way through to the ballot, and chances are only four in ten that the initiative will be approved. Nevertheless, the popularity of initiatives has grown dramatically in recent years.

A referendum is a procedure for referring or submitting measures already passed by a legislative body to the electorate, for approval or rejection. Bond issues for new schools, highways, and pollution control are typical examples of measures passed by local government and then placed before the general electorate for final action.

Under the 1976 lobby law, IRS regulations recognize that in referenda, initiatives, and similar procedures, the public itself is the legislature. Therefore, communications to the public that refer to an initiative or referendum are treated as direct lobbying, not grassroots lobbying. Nonprofits' ceiling for spending on direct lobbying is four times as much as the ceiling on grassroots lobbying. It follows that nonprofits have more latitude to lobby on behalf of an initiative or a referendum than they would have had if (as some had feared) the final IRS regulations had said that such lobbying is grassroots lobbying. This means that a nonprofit—in a newspaper ad, for example—can refer to a specific initiative or referendum, reflect a view on the proposal, and urge readers not only to vote for or against the initiative or referendum but also to ask their neighbors to do likewise. The nonprofit can then charge all of it as direct lobbying. (Under

IRS regulations, such activities aimed at the general public on legislation other than initiatives, referenda, and similar procedures are considered grassroots lobbying and are therefore subject to the lower expenditure limit.)

It is clear that initiatives, referenda, and similar processes provide an opportunity for nonprofit lobbying that has been largely overlooked until recently. All states have provisions of some kind permitting citizens to vote directly on legislation. The liberal IRS rules regarding nonprofit lobbying on initiatives and referenda should provide enormously increased incentives for nonprofits to enter into this arena.

Voter Education by Nonprofits During a Political Campaign

Nonprofits sometimes confuse working for the election of a political candidate with lobbying. These two kinds of activity are in fact very different. It is perfectly legal (and highly appropriate) for a nonprofit to work for the passage of a particular piece of legislation, during a political campaign or at any other time. Working for the election of a particular political candidate, however, federal, state, or local—is strictly prohibited and is cause for the nonprofit to lose its tax-exempt status.

In the past, there was considerable uncertainty about the voter-education activities that nonprofits could conduct during a political campaign without jeopardizing their tax-exempt status. That uncertainty had grown out of 1954 legislation by Congress to the effect that a 501(c)(3) organization must "not participate in, or intervene in (including publishing or distributing statements), any political campaign on behalf of any

candidate for public office." The problem for nonprofits was that Congress had not clarified this language, and the IRS had published no regulations. To clarify the latitude available to nonprofits to carry out voter-education activities, INDEPENDENT SECTOR sought letter rulings by the IRS. Letter rulings state how the IRS applies the tax law and regulations to particular circumstances. Although they formally bind the IRS only in the case of the individual organization that receives the letter ruling, they do provide guidance on IRS thinking about similar situations with other organizations. Two rulings received in 1980 have provided extremely important guidance.

While a 501(c)(3) group cannot work on behalf of or against candidates, the IRS letter rulings to INDEPENDENT SECTOR indicate that there are a number of other voter activities that it can legally engage in.

Electioneering

A 501(c)(3) organization cannot endorse, contribute to, work for, or otherwise support a candidate for public office, nor can it oppose one. This in no way prohibits officers, individual members, or employees from participating, provided that they say or do everything as private citizens and not as spokespersons for the organization or while using the organization's resources. If they choose to identify themselves with the organization, they must make it plain that they are speaking solely for themselves and not for the organization. If members do not identify themselves with the organization but the media do, the members have done nothing wrong.

Candidates' Statements

It is entirely proper for a nonprofit to inform candidates of its positions on particular issues and to urge them to go on record, pledging their support of those positions. Such action from candidates is often very helpful in getting legislation enacted that is favored by nonprofits. Such statements become useful to nonprofits after an election is over because they may distribute such statements broadly after the election.

Candidates may distribute their responses both to the nonprofit and to the general public. Nonprofits, however, do not have the same freedom. They may not publish or distribute statements by candidates except as nonpartisan "questionnaires" (discussed in the following paragraph) or as part of bona fide news reports. This includes candidates' statements to the media, to the general public, and to nonprofit organizations. The same applies to any statement volunteered by the candidate, even if a nonprofit has not solicited the statement. The candidate may distribute this statement at will, but the nonprofit may not until after the election.

Questionnaires

Nonprofits with a broad range of concerns can safely disseminate responses from questionnaires. The questions must cover a broad range of subjects, be framed without bias, and be given to all candidates for office.

If a nonprofit has a very narrow focus, however, questionnaires may pose a problem. The IRS takes the position that a nonprofit's narrowness of focus implies endorsement of candidates whose replies are favorable to the questions posed. The same applies when candidates are asked to respond to a nonprofit's position paper. Unless you are certain that your organization clearly qualifies as covering a broad range of issues, your organization should avoid disseminating replies from questionnaires.

Voting Records

Many nonprofits follow the useful practice of telling their members how each member of a legislature has voted on a key issue. This device shows who should be thanked and who needs to be persuaded and is a critically important tool in moving legislation forward. There is no legal problem with this practice, provided that if the information is presented and disseminated during the campaign it is done in the same manner as it is at other times. In presenting the results, it is important not to say "voted for us" or anything similar. Just say that the legislator voted for or against the measure. (The IRS has permitted the use of a plus (+) or a minus (-) to indicate whether a legislator has voted in accord with the organization's position.)

A problem arises if an organization waits to disseminate voting records until a campaign is under way. If your organization has followed the practice of disseminating voting records as votes occur throughout the year, then you are safe in publishing the record of a vote that occurs during a campaign. If, however, your organization has not published records regularly throughout the year, your group may not, during the campaign, publish a recap of the legislative votes throughout the legislative session. That is permissible, however, after the election.

Public Forums

Nonprofits may invite candidates to meetings or to public forums sponsored by the organizations, in order to get the candidates' views on subjects of particular interest. The invitation must be extended to "all serious candidates." It is best to write to them all simultaneously and to use identical language in the invitations. It is not necessary that all candidates attend.

Even-handedness must be maintained in promoting and holding such a meeting or forum. The nonprofit should not state its views or comment on those of the candidates. If there is a question-and-answer period, each candidate must be given an equal opportunity to answer questions, and the moderator should strive to ensure balance.

Speeches or other remarks by candidates at the forum may be published as news items in the nonprofit's newsletter, if it is published regularly and if its circulation is limited to the organization's normal distribution patterns. All candidates must be given an equal opportunity to appear, and the news stories must be presented without editorial comment.

Testimony on Party Platforms

As part of a lobbying effort, nonprofits may testify before party platform committees at the national, state, or local levels of government. Responses to testimony may be reported in regularly published newsletters. Both parties' platform committees should receive copies of the testimony. Any account of the testimony and responses may be reported in a regularly scheduled publication.

Issue Briefings and Candidates' Statements

Issue briefings for candidates must be extended to all the candidates running for a particular office. A candidate may publish a position paper or statement on the issue, but a nonprofit may not circulate the candidate's statement to the media, the general public, or the nonprofit's members until after the election.

Membership Lists

The nonprofit may *sell, trade,* or *rent its* list to others, including candidates for office. If it does so, all candidates must be aware of the opportunity and be given the same access. An organization that *gives* or *lends* its membership list to a candidate is in effect making an illegal campaign contribution. To stay within the law, the group must be paid fair value in return.

Indirect Lobbying Through a 501(c)(4) Organization

Some nonprofits have chosen to enlarge and strengthen their lobbying abilities by establishing 501(c)(4) organizations, thereby taking advantage of a 1983 U.S. Supreme Court decision. *Regan* v. *Taxation With Representation of Washington*, said that the First Amendment requires that 501(c)(3) organizations be permitted to lobby indirectly through 501(c)(4) organizations.

Nonprofits—501(c)(3) organizations—are limited by law as to the amount they may spend on lobbying without penalty (see Chapter 9). Organizations that are tax-exempt under Section 501(c)(4) do not have limitations on lobbying on behalf of their exempt purpose. Charitable contributions to 501(c)(4) organizations, however, are not tax-deductible.

Before the *Regan* v. *Taxation With Representation of Washington* decision, it had never been entirely clear to what extent a nonprofit could control the actions of a lobbying affiliate. As a result of this uncertainty, very few nonprofits had set up 501(c)(4) organizations to indirectly broaden their lobbying outreach. The Supreme Court decision made clear that all the IRS can require by way of separation between a nonprofit and its 501(c)(4) lobbying affiliate is "that the affiliate be separately incorporated" and that it "keep records adequate to show that tax-deductible contributions are not used to pay for lobbying" *(Regan* v. *Taxation With Representation of Washington*, 1983).

A nonprofit can therefore control the activities of, and the legislative position taken by, its lobbying [501(c)(4)] affiliate. It is clear that a nonprofit and a 501(c)(4) affiliate may have identical priorities and boards of directors, and they may share personnel, office space, and facilities. In effect, a 501(c)(3) organization can set up and run a 501(c)(4) organization if the latter can raise its own hard money—that is, attract nondeductible contributions. The Supreme Court case should make the IRS very reluctant to push, on audit, the issue of a nonprofit's lobbying indirectly through a 501(c)(4) organization simply because the nonprofit controls it. But the 501(c)(4) organization must be run as a separate legal entity and must pay all its costs with nondeductible funds. The IRS can and does monitor that requirement closely. Therefore, it is important for the

501(c)(3) organization and the 501(c)(4) group to keep good records, showing that they properly divide costs for office space, staff time, equipment, and so on, so that the 501(c)(3) organization does not subsidize the 501(c)(4) organization.

For the vast majority of 501(c)(3) organizations, the 1976 lobby law provides all the lobbying latitude needed. Those groups that would like more lobbying conducted in their areas of interest should consider setting up a 501(c)(4) affiliate. Care will be needed, however, in keeping the two groups clearly separate, and contributors must be told that gifts to the affiliate are not deductible as charitable contributions.

Individual and Political Action Committee (PAC) Contributions to Political Campaigns

A 501(c)(3) organization may not endorse, work for, pay the costs of, or otherwise support or oppose a candidate for public office. But, again, this in no way prohibits any of the nonprofit's officers, individual members, or employees from participating in elections, provided anything they say or do is done as private citizens and not as spokespersons for the nonprofit. If they choose to identify themselves with the organization, they must make it clear that they are speaking solely for themselves and not for the organization. If they do not identify themselves with the nonprofit but the media does, they have done nothing wrong. However, to protect the organization, the individuals should clarify that the media's characterization is incorrect.

Organizations that are tax-exempt under Section 501(c)(3) of the Internal Revenue Code are not permitted to establish political action committees (PACs). PACs are committees that raise or disburse money in federal election campaigns. They have become vehicles for the political involvement of supporters of unions, corporations, and other groups. PACs have been set up by a number of 501(c)(4) organizations. There is nothing to prohibit a 501(c)(3) from setting up a 501(c)(4), which in turn may set up a PAC, provided that the 501(c)(3) does not financially support either the 501(c)(4) or the PAC.

Under federal election law, 501(c)(4) groups cannot make contributions to federal candidates. Under recent Supreme Court rulings, however, *(Federal Election Commission* v. *Massachusetts Citizens for Life Inc., Dec. 15, 1986* and *Austin* v. *Michigan Chamber of Commerce, March 27, 1990)* a 501(c)(4) organization that gets no union or business money, operates entirely independently of any campaign, and meets other standards can make independent contributions for or against a candidate. Under those rulings, a 501(c)(4) organization is allowed to use dues and contributions for independent political spending without being obliged to establish a PAC and solicit funds for it separately. Direct contributions to federal candidates remain impermissible, as do coordinated efforts with a campaign. The independent expenditures must be reported to the Federal Election Commission. A 501(c)(4) organization that makes independent expenditures (or operates in a state that permits corporate contributions) is subject, under Internal Revenue Code Section 527, to taxation on its investment income, to the extent of its campaign expenditures and contributions.

OMB Circular A-122—Restrictions on Nonprofits That Lobby and Receive Federal Funds

Charities are prohibited from using any federal funds for legislative lobbying and electioneering. However, they are not restricted from using private resources to lobby. The use of private resources for lobbying are guided by the IRS rules discussed in this book.

Cost principles are general rules that govern whether and under what circumstances the government will pay for costs incurred by contractors and grantees. In 1984, the Office of Management and Budget (OMB) issued cost principles covering most nonprofits on the prohibition of lobbying with federal grants. Since that time, rules have been developed that consistently prohibit any recipient of federal grants, contracts, or cooperative agreements from using such funds for lobbying or electioneering.

Most nonprofit federal grantees are covered by OMB Circular A-122, Cost Principles for Nonprofit Organizations. Colleges and universities are governed by OMB Circular A-21; hospital rules are contained in "Principles for Determining Costs Applicable to Research and Development under Grants and Contracts with Hospitals" (45 CFR part 74, Appendix E). For commercial entities with contracts, cost principles are provided in the Federal Acquisition Regulation (FAR).

There are only two differences between cost principles for grantees and contractors. First, it is unallowable for contractors to use federal funds to lobby at the local level; such a prohibition is not placed on grantees. Second, there are financial penalties that can be assessed against contractors in certain situations that cannot be levied against grantees.

Lobbying and Political Activity Provisions of Circular A-122

As a condition of obtaining federal grant, grantees are required to make certain that none of those funds are used for lobbying or political activity, as defined by OMB. Grantees are subject to audits to verify that grant funds have not been used either directly or indirectly for any unallowable expenses, such as lobbying. Using federal grant funds for unallowable expenses can result in suspension of the grant, debarment from future grants, and repayment of money.

Circular A-122, as well as the other circulars and the FAR, prohibit using federal funds for:

- Any attempt to influence the introduction, enactment or modification of federal or state legislation either through direct communications or through indirect, grassroots efforts such as media or letter writing campaigns;
- Legislation liaison activities, which includes attending legislative hearings, or gathering or analyzing legislation when done in support of or in "knowing preparation" for a lobbying effort;
- Any attempt to influence the outcome of federal, state, or local elections, referenda, initiatives, or similar procedures through contributions, endorsements or other approaches; and
- Establishing, administering, contributing to, or paying the expenses of a political party, campaign, political action committee,

or other organization established for influencing the outcome of an election.

The distinction between grants and contracts is that for the first two points—prohibiting lobbying and legislative liaison activities—the prohibition on grants is for federal and state legislation, whereas for contractors it also includes local legislation. In earlier drafts of Circular A-122, there were proposals to include local legislation. But OMB concluded that it was too hard to distinguish whether a communications with a city or county office was lobbying since many local offices perform both executive and legislative functions.

What Is Not Lobbying?

OMB Circular A-122 exempts the following three activities from its list of unallowable lobbying activities:

- Providing technical and factual information in response to a "documented" request, such as a notice in a government publication requesting testimony or statements for the record, on a topic directly related to the performance of a grant, contract, or other agreement. The information must be readily obtainable and easily put into a deliverable form;
- Lobbying at the state level in order to directly reduce the costs or avoid material impairment of the organization's authority to perform the grant, contract, or agreement. Lobbying for the purpose of improving performance is not exempt; and

- Anything specifically authorized by statute to be undertaken with funds from the grant, contract, or other agreement.

Circular A-122 does not designate what federal grant funds can be used for—only what is unallowable. Even if something is not prohibited, it does not mean that it is allowable. It must also be consistent with the purposes of the grant. A grantee should contact the awarding federal agency to discuss specific expenditures to determine whether they will be allowable under the grant. That should help a charity clarify, from the outset, any ambiguity about expenditures of federal funds.

Amount of Lobbying Permitted

Federal cost principles, such as Circular A-122, place no restrictions on the amount of lobbying that may be undertaken, as long as none of the lobbying costs, either direct or indirect, are done with funds obtained through a federal grant or contract, subgrant or subcontract. Indirect costs, such as overhead, include those costs that are incurred for common or joint objectives and which cannot readily be assigned to a particular program or activity.

Record Keeping and Reporting

Circular A-122 requires grantees to maintain adequate records and refers them to its Circular A-110 as a source of further information.

To ensure that activities funded by federal awards do not bear more than their fair share of *indirect costs* (managers' salaries, support services, utilities, and so

on), the charitable organization annually negotiates with the awarding federal agency the manner in which indirect costs are to be determined and allocated. An organization receiving grants, contracts, or subawards from more than one agency negotiates with the agency that is making the largest dollar volume of awards and then applies the results to the awards from other agencies.

In advance of other negotiation, the organization submits a formal proposal, which forms the basis for negotiation. Any gray areas between organization and agency are resolved during negotiation and may not be reopened during audit.

A charity's indirect-cost proposal must identify total lobbying costs to be included during the award. Thus lobbying conducted by a group with its private funds must be identified.

Each direct-cost employee who expects to allocate more than 25 percent of his or her time to lobbying or lobbying support during any month is required to keep a time log for that month.

Lobbying with Private Foundation Grants and Corporate Contributions

Nonprofits are not disqualified from lobbying because they receive foundation funds, but nonprofits and, even more, foundations have been slow to recognize and act on this fact. While grant funds from a private foundation to a nonprofit must not be earmarked for lobbying, it is perfectly legal for the nonprofit to use unearmarked foundation funds to lobby. Foundation funds are considered to be earmarked only if there has been an oral or written agreement that the grant will be used for specific purposes. If there is no oral or written agreement and the nonprofit controls how the grant funds are used, then it may lobby with those general-purpose grant dollars.

The IRS regulations have set up a highly protective system for grants by private foundations to nonprofits that lobby. The regulations apply to all grants for nonprofits, and they should remove any remaining uncertainty among foundations about granting funds to nonprofits that elect to come under the 1976 lobby law. Under these rules, a foundation may, without incurring a penalty tax, make a general-purpose grant to a nonprofit that lobbies and may make a grant to support a specific project that includes lobbying, as long as its own grant is less than the amount budgeted for the nonlobbying parts of the project. For example (to repeat a scenario described in Chapter 9), if a specific project has a $200,000 budget, of which $20,000 is to be spent for lobbying, then a private foundation may give the project up to $180,000 (the part of the project budget allocated to nonlobbying uses). The fact that other private foundations have already made grants for the project need not be taken into account in considering how much a private foundation can give. See Chapter 9 for a more detailed discussion.

The regulations make clear that the foundation can rely on statements by the prospective grantee as to the lobbying budget for a project, unless it knows or has reason to know that the statements are false. The regulations also make clear that, so long as the grantor foundation complies with these standards when it makes the grant, it will not be held to

have made a taxable lobbying expenditure because the nonprofit violates the assurances it gave when seeking the grant.

There are other important areas associated with legislation that are not considered lobbying, where it is permissible for nonprofits to use earmarked foundation funds. They include nonpartisan analysis or research and provision of technical advice or assistance to a governmental or legislative body in response to a written request from that body. Nonprofits may devote an unlimited amount of their activity to providing such technical advice or assistance to a governmental or legislative body in response to a written request from that body, and they can provide nonpartisan analysis or research even though such matters relate to pending legislation. All of that activity may be fully funded by foundations.

The IRS regulations are also clear that a nonprofit may use foundation funds to furnish results of analysis or research on legislative issues, if it presents the facts fully and fairly enough so that the audience can form independent opinions. The regulations make clear that research and analysis need not be neutral or objective to fall within this nonpartisan exclusion. The exclusion also covers research or analysis that takes a direct position on the merits of legislation, as long as the organization presents facts fully and fairly, makes the material generally available, and does not include a direct call to the reader to contact legislators.

Nonprofits that have elected to come under the 1976 lobby law have occasionally found that foundations have been "scared off" by the fact that the nonprofit has elected to come under the provisions of that legislation. Some foundations fear that a general-purpose grant to a nonprofit that has been elected might make them subject to a tax penalty. The IRS regulations, which codified a 1977 letter ruling to the McIntosh Foundation, make clear that such fears are unfounded. The regulations hold that general-support grants to nonprofits that have elected to come under the 1976 lobby law (like those nonprofits that have not elected) do not constitute taxable expenditures if the grants are not earmarked, and if there is no written or oral agreement that the nonprofit will use the grants for specific lobbying purposes. Regulations based on the McIntosh Ruling should allay any remaining fears of foundations regarding general-purpose grants to nonprofits that elect.

Nonprofits may receive grants earmarked for lobbying from community foundations. Community foundations are tax-exempt under Section 501(c)(3) of the Internal Revenue Code and are not treated as private foundations so they are permitted the same lobbying latitude as other nonprofits. For example, a community foundation that has elected to come under the 1976 lobby law may spend funds to lobby. It may also grant earmarked funds to a nonprofit group for lobbying, up to the limits permitted by law. A community foundation's grant, earmarked for lobbying, would count against the community foundation's own lobbying ceiling. A community foundation may receive earmarked personal funds for lobbying only if the funds are not deducted by the donor from his or her taxes.

There are other important ways in which private foundation funds can be used to lobby. Foundations may fund self-defense direct lobbying by a nonprofit if the legislation would directly affect the foundation. For example, if a nonprofit were conducting direct lobbying in support of increased charitable tax incentives that would affect contributions to foundations, it would be permissible for the foundation to fund that activity.

There is much more latitude for making grants to nonprofits that lobby than many believe. A number of foundations have liberalized their policies for granting funds to nonprofits that lobby, and nonprofits are well served by this enlightened view.

Nonprofits have never actively pursued corporations to fund lobbying activities, although a growing number of corporations are supporting nonprofits that lobby aggressively for their causes and clients. A nonprofit may use corporate or personal contributions to lobby if the contributions are not earmarked for lobbying.

Reporting Lobbying Expenditures to the IRS

Organizations that lobby (except churches, associations of churches, and integrated auxiliaries) are required to report their lobbying expenditures to the IRS on Form 990. Record keeping and reporting requirements for organizations that elect to come under the 1976 lobby law are somewhat different from requirements for those that fall under the substantiality test. For electing organizations they are simpler.

All nonprofits, whether they elect or not, have to report annually to the IRS how much they spend on lobbying. The only additional information required of electing organizations is to calculate their ceilings and state how much of their lobbying is grassroots (for example, aimed at getting the general public to lobby legislators). Electing organizations, unlike those subject to the substantiality test, are not required to include detailed descriptions of their lobbying activities.

For groups that have not elected, the detailed description that the group is required to attach asks, for example, whether the organization lobbied through the use of volunteers and paid staff, whether it used media advertisements, legislators, rallies, and a number of other activities. The detailed description also must include information on the amount of noncompensation plus compensation expenses incurred for each activity.

Both types of organizations do have to maintain records. If they are audited, they will be required to substantiate what they have reported on Form 990. Electing and nonelecting organizations need systems for recording how much they spend on lobbying.

The IRS will accept any reasonable method of doing this. For example, you may use a sampling, instead of complete time records, to estimate how much time your staff spends on lobbying activity. If the sample periods are generally representative of how you use most of your time, you might want to pick out a two-week period each quarter and keep track of your activities, in 30 minute segments, to determine how much of your activities constitutes lobbying. In estimating your lobbying expenditures each quarter, you would simply make adjustments on the basis of your in-depth two-week assessments. Overhead costs related to your lobbying expenditures must also be reported.

The main point is that you should make a good-faith effort to keep track of your lobbying expenditures. You may want to develop a form, which would include such information as the date, the nature of the activity (visit with a legislator, development of an action alert, telephone calls to your members urging action), and whether it represented direct or grassroots lobbying. The extent to which you want to keep a regular record of your lobbying activities will depend on how representative your sample assessment is and on whether you can make reasonably close general estimates from that assessment without keeping more detailed records.

Registering and Filing Reports Under the Lobbying Disclosure Act of 1995

The Lobbying Disclosure Act took effect January 1, 1996, and it may require your organization to register and file reports.

If your organization has at least one employee who devotes at least 20 percent of his or her time to "lobbying activities" *and* spends $20,000 or more every six months on such activities, your organization is required to register and file reports under the Act. The Act has two different definitions of lobbying activities and as a result of extensive lobbying by INDEPENDENT SECTOR and other organizations, you can choose which definition to apply to your organization.

INDEPENDENT SECTOR was concerned that the Lobbying Disclosure Act would define lobbying quite differently from the definitions for nonprofit lobbying under the 1976 lobby law, with the result that nonprofits would have to keep two "sets of books." One set, for reporting to the

IRS, the other for reporting to the House and Senate under the Lobbying Disclosure Act. The Lobbying Disclosure Act definitions of lobbying are quite different from the IRS rules, but fortunately, those nonprofits that have elected to come under the provisions of the 1976 lobby law, can use the 1976 law definitions to report their lobbying under the Lobbying Disclosure Act. Nonprofits that have elected under the 1976 rules and have disclosed to the House and Senate their lobbying based on the 1976 rules, have not found the reporting to be onerous. On the other hand, groups that have not elected have the double burden of reporting to the House and Senate under Lobbying Disclosure Act definitions and reporting to the IRS under the rules that apply to a "non-electing" nonprofit. This clearly is one more very good reason for a nonprofit to elect to come under the 1976 rules, in addition to the advantages spelled out in Chapter 9.

Non-electing nonprofits that are subject to the definitions under the Lobbying Disclosure Act must report their "lobbying contacts" plus planning, research, and other background activities in support of such contacts. The Lobbying Disclosure Act defines lobbying contacts as oral or written contacts by an employee/lobbyist with members of Congress and their staffs, *and* with senior-level Executive Branch officials, concerning: (a) influencing federal legislation; (b) influencing federal rules and regulations, executive orders, and other policy positions; (c) negotiation, award or administration of federal programs, policies, contracts, grants, loans, permits, or licenses; and (d) nominations subject to Senate

confirmation. There are 19 exceptions, such as making speeches, publishing articles, and submitting Congressional testimony. Note that the new Act's definition applies only to lobbying activities related to the *federal government.*

Here is how you determine whether your lobbying expenditures total $20,000 or more in a six-month period:

The new Lobbying Disclosure Act simply requires you to make a "good faith estimate" of lobbying expenses. The lawmakers said this means you should have "a reasonable estimating system in place" and follow it. You should allocate salary and general overhead costs to lobbying based on the percentage of time your professional staff devotes to "lobbying activities," and add other direct costs of lobbying such as printing, postage, and out-of-pocket expenses. You may want to run more precise calculations if you need to prove your expenditures fall beneath the threshold described above so that you don't have to register.

If you are reporting your lobbying expenditures to the IRS based on the 1976 lobby law, you would follow the information in Chapter 9 to determine how to report that same information to comply with the Lobbying Disclosure Act. So, if, under the IRS rules your lobbying expenditures are more than $20,000 during a six-month period *and* you have an employee who spends more than 20 percent of his or her time lobbying during that period, you would have to register and report.

The reports of your expenditures are for specific six-month periods: January through June and July through December.

If your organization's lobbying expenditures require registering under the

Act, you must file a registration statement with the Senate and House within 45 days after an employee/lobbyist—makes or is employed to make—a "lobbying contact," and then file semi-annual reports. To obtain a copy of the registration statement, Form LD-1, contact:

> Secretary of the Senate
> Office of Public Records
> 232 Hart Senate Office Building
> Washington, DC 20510
>
> or
>
> Clerk of the House of Representatives
> Legislative Resource Center
> 1036 Longworth House
>   Office Building
> Washington, DC 20515

You must file Form LD-1 with both offices.

If you elect to come under the provisions of the 1976 lobby law, the election is retroactive to January 1 of the year for which it is made. It is probably permissible for any organization that makes the election during the year to comply with the Lobbying Disclosure Act using the tax law expenditures for that year.

Rules for Lawmaker Gifts and Entertainment

The U.S. Senate and House of Representatives have rules that sharply limit the acceptance of gifts, entertainment, and transportation by members of Congress, their staffs and other congressional employees. The new rules tend to level somewhat the political playing field, since nonprofits have not been able—even if they had wanted—to match corporations in bestowing gifts and entertainment for legislative access or influence.

An individual can only provide a Senator, Representative or staff member with a gift (or meal) worth less than $50. Multiple gifts from one source cannot total more than $100 per year.

Both Senate and House rules except items of nominal value such as caps or t-shirts—as well as coffee and doughnuts, hors d'oeuvres, or other "minimal" refreshments. They also may except gifts from family members or close personal friends. The rules also except commemorative plaques and trophies.

You can still invite a Senator, Representative, or staffer to appear or speak at your convention, conference or nonprofit event in an official capacity, and pay for their "necessary transportation, lodging and related expenses." Whatever meals, concerts, or other entertainment you provide for your congressional guest should be an "integral part of the event." You cannot provide your guest with recreational opportunities incidental to the event.

Moreover, you cannot cover travel costs for a congressional lawmaker or aide to take part in "substantially recreational" events such as celebrity golf tournaments or other nonprofit outings.

As before, you cannot offer honoraria to congressional members or aides. But you can still contribute, instead, to nonprofits they designate.

For additional information contact the House Committee on Standards of Office Conduct, HT-2 Capitol Building, Washington, DC 20515, 202/225-7103, or the Senate Ethics Committee, 220 Hart Senate Office Building, Washington, DC 20510, 202/224-2981.

Part Three

Why Lobby In The Public Interest?

For many people, the idea of being a "lobbyist" is not very appealing. As John Sparks writes in this part, when he was young, his image of a lobbyist was "a kind of specialized crook who wore good clothes and knew famous people in Washington." For others such as Bev Adcock, the idea of being a lobbyist never even crossed their minds.

But as the following essays make clear, being a public interest lobbyist can be an extremely effective way for people to live out their values and feel that they are having an impact on people and causes they care about. Six people who have very different causes and experiences write about how they got into lobbying. They explain how lobbying has helped their causes, their organizations, *and* their careers, many saying that lobbying has been the most rewarding, stimulating work they have done in their lives. Many also offer insights about how to be an effective lobbyist that come from long experience.

This is particularly true of David Cohen's essay. David believes so strongly in public interest lobbying that he helped start a national organization devoted to helping people do it—The Advocacy Institute. He contends that lobbying is important not just to win policies that can help many people, but also "to help balance the many special interests that, naturally enough, push policy in ways that benefit narrow parts of the population." He explains that public interest lobbyists often bring to the process the views of people who are excluded. "Finding ways to organize and amplify the voices of your members and constituents is one of the most satisfying—and challenging—aspects of being a public interest lobbyist. Seeing people who never participated in anything become engaged and empowering themselves—seeing their lives change—is extremely gratifying."

For Bev Adcock, the key was trying to change the life of one person: a child named Becky who had severe disabilities. "As I fought for changes that would make Becky's life better, I kept running into problems that could only be solved by changing the system." Eventually, Adcock came to realize that "changing systems is the best way to affect the lives of thousands of people at once." She adds that becoming a lobbyist "has been a marvelous journey."

Hilda Robbins, a life-long volunteer, also became a lobbyist after trying to help a few individuals whose lives were being wasted in a state mental hospital. She started by trying to create a single "half-way house" that would allow a handful of patients to return to their communities. But someone asked her, "What about all the patients at her state's 18 other mental hospitals?" That question helped change her life, embarking her on a 40-year career as a lobbyist for mentally ill people across the country. She does lobbying because "it is the most effective, dramatic, exhilarating, rewarding and usually most practical way" to help people.

For John Sparks, the key was not a decision to become a lobbyist, but to apply his lobbying skills to the public interest. Just being a lobbyist for a series of clients was becoming both boring and dispiriting for him. "I didn't have a lust for widget promotion," he writes. But then he went to work for the organization that lobbies for the country's symphony and chamber orchestras. He quickly was immersed in fighting attempts to cut off public funding for all of the arts. He has found great passion for this work, not only because he cares about music and the arts, but also because he believes in this country's democratic process. He writes that those who were trying to cut off public support for the arts were "totally corrupting" the democratic process through their "demagoguery, distortion, and outright fiction."

Eden Fisher Durbin came to lobbying because it gave her a way to help people that didn't involve providing direct services, which requires an "extraordinary gift" and patience that she found she simply did not have. She learned that lobbying can help those who can provide direct services. She tells the story of lobbying against legislation that threatened to prevent her organization—the YMCA—from doing something that it was doing very well: providing child care for school-age children across the country. "To ensure the development of sound programs," she writes, "service providers should share their knowledge and understanding" with those who pass laws and set policies.

Dorothy Johnson's story points out how an organization like hers—the Council of Michigan Foundations—often must get involved in lobbying to accomplish its mission. This association of foundations wanted to make sure that every community in the state could support and had access to a "community foundation." But state law provided no tax incentives for charitable gifts to community foundations. Through lobbying, the Council changed the law, a change that has stimulated a big expansion in Michigan's community foundations. She asks a simple but important question: "If we do not speak for ourselves, who will? In whatever field in which we work—education, the arts, social well-being, the environment, philanthropy—we are the experts."

What it all comes down to, writes David Cohen, is the immense satisfaction of being part of a process that helps society "move from 'what is' to 'what ought to be,' carrying out the values you believe in and stand for. As I reflect on my lobbying career, it is the sense that I was part of some extraordinary changes—changes that have brought this country a little closer to what it 'ought to be'—that makes me proud that I chose this career."

How I Became a Nonprofit Lobbyist

by Bev Adcock, Executive Director
The Arc of Utah

"When I grow up, I want to be a nonprofit lobbyist," were words that never came out of my mouth as a child. Until 1980, when I started working for The Arc (a nonprofit organization that advocates for people with mental retardation and their families), I never thought about lobbying at all. In fact, I worked for The Arc for two years before I really understood why they did what they did. It was a child that made it all clear.

"I need to go visit a two-year old who's living in a nursing home." I feel the same horror now at those words that I did when a co-worker from The Arc said them to me almost 16 years ago. I went with her to visit this child and in a few short minutes, the course of my life changed forever.

Becky was two and lived in 68 different places before ending up in the nursing home. Given up for adoption by her birth mother, Becky was dropped from the adoption lists when they discovered she had disabilities. Profound mental retardation, cerebral palsy, and seizures were only a few of her problems. She was fed through a stomach tube, was considered blind and deaf and screamed if anyone touched her. The nursing home solved this last problem by touching her as little as possible and leaving her alone in a dark room for most of each day.

I was horrified that anyone would treat a child this way and I wanted to stop it. My co-worker had been asked to find a volunteer advocate for Becky. After one look, I knew I wanted the job.

Meeting Becky was really the beginning of my lobbying career. At first, my focus was purely on changing things for Becky, but over time I learned that much of what was wrong in her life was wrong for a lot of other people with disabilities too. I became more and more angry at a child care system that didn't seem to care about children.

At first, I spent time on issues that just affected Becky. Why had her caseworker not seen her since she was six months old? Why had they assumed she was blind and deaf instead of testing her to find out for sure?

As time passed, however, I started to wonder about the whole system. Why didn't they require caseworkers to visit their kids regularly to make sure they were all right? If a child had disabilities, why weren't they treated?

What had started out as a crusade to fix things for this child I had grown to love became a need to make sure no other child got treated the same way. The more I learned about the "child protective" system that was intended to help kids, the more I believed the system itself was something from which children needed to be protected.

As I fought for changes that would make Becky's life better, I kept running into problems that could only be solved by changing the system. Before I knew it, I was lobbying, although I certainly didn't think about it in those terms! I was just trying to help Becky. The fact that I had to talk to state employees and elected officials to change things for her was just part of the process.

As Becky's life changed, my interests grew. When Becky was moved from the nursing home to a state institution, I had to learn how the system worked and how to change it. I also started looking at issues that didn't affect Becky yet, but would eventually, like school and adult services. As I looked ahead at what Becky would face as she grew older, I saw a lot more things that needed to be changed. There didn't seem to be a place to stop.

I have worked on a lot of issues in the 16 years since I first saw Becky in that nursing home. But the image of that small child lying alone, dirty and in the dark, remains etched in my heart. It has driven me to fight to keep children in families and out of nursing homes and institutions. It has forced me to work to change the system so neglect is not an accepted part of the treatment of people with disabilities. It has made me care about issues like family support, special education, quality residential programs, training of direct care staff, and services for adults. It has even, to my surprise, involved me in lobbying local, state, and federal legislators.

For me, lobbying will always be about Becky. Through my experiences with her, I learned that changing systems is the best way to affect the lives of thousands of people at once. But we must never lose sight of the individuals in that system. Although she died in 1987, I still measure proposed changes in the law by how they would affect her if she were still here. Would her life be better or worse if proposed legislation passed?

Lobbying is nothing more than trying to help someone understand an issue from my viewpoint. Of course, that's easier if they actually want to know what I think, but even if they don't, I have to find a way to get the message across. Since my goal is to help them understand the impact on people with mental retardation and other disabilities, it helps that I can use Becky and my other friends with disabilities as examples. My job is to make the human impact real to those I am lobbying.

My experiences with Becky changed the course of my life forever. While lobbying for a nonprofit wasn't the direction I expected to take, it has been a marvelous journey. I started out to make the world a better place for Becky because I cared about this one child. Her gift to me was a career that gives me a chance to make the world a better place for all of us.

Thoughts about Lobbying by Volunteers

by Hilda H. Robbins, Volunteer Lobbyist

I first became aware of such a thing as "advocacy" and "social action" in 1954, when I tried to convince the executive director of the Mental Health Association of Southeastern Pennsylvania to finance and operate what was then called a "half-way house." I was doing volunteer work with long-term patients at a state hospital, patients I knew should not have been in the hospital.

The executive, Richard Hunter, explained gently and convincingly that supporting one half-way house for six or eight patients would be commendable. But he challenged me with the idea that the Association could be more effective convincing the state legislature to support many out-of-hospital residences, which would allow patients from all 19 state mental hospitals to have a better life. I was sold on the concept, and immediately began working on that goal. In the early 1950s I never thought I'd become a lobbyist for the rest of my life, nor that I would get more satisfaction from this volunteer activity than any real "career" I was considering.

Why do I lobby? Very simply, because it is the most effective, dramatic, exhilarating, rewarding and usually the most practical way to cause change or stop unwanted change. Lobbying is an especially important role for volunteers, who can be extremely effective advocates.

The most satisfying and exhilarating lobbying effort I've been involved with shows why lobbying by a charity's volunteers and staff is so important. It involved the re-authorization of the Community Mental Health Centers Act in 1975. The act was the centerpiece of the movement to return patients to their communities. But it had been vetoed for the second time by President Ford.

The key was the Senate. The coalition fighting for the Act identified every senator who didn't either strongly support or oppose the bill. Each senator was assigned to someone. It wasn't easy getting in to see them, but our lobbyists were so intent on getting the message directly to the senators that we hung around in the halls and waited in offices for hours just to get a one-on-one discussion and commitment. We met each night to plan strategy. All this intense work of volunteers and staff paid off when we easily got the two-thirds vote we needed to override the veto. We celebrated!

In my many years as a volunteer for the National Association for Mental Health, I often made speeches to our affiliates in hundreds of cities. I never failed to make two forceful points. The first reminded people what it takes to be an effective advocacy agency. I often summarized the succinct requirements of John Gardner, the founder of Common Cause and INDEPENDENT SECTOR:

1. Have stamina and persistence;
2. Have a narrow focus;
3. Have accurate knowledge;
4. Have a stable financial base;
5. Have credibility;
6. Have visibility; and
7. Be able to work with other groups.

The second point I made summarized how to lobby, especially for volunteers. What I hoped to communicate was that, by following a few simple rules, anyone can lobby. You do not have to be a professional. These rules included:

1. Keep your letter short and accurate. Use your personal letterhead. Ask the person you are lobbying some specific question that requires a response.
2. Don't shy away from using a personal experience. For example: "My aunt was in a state mental hospital for 33 miserable, un-therapeutic years. This is not only inhuman but costly and totally unnecessary." (I never hesitated to use my personal experience with mental illness when appropriate.)
3. Establish a good relationship with everyone in a Congressperson's office, especially the appointment secretary and the legislative assistant. Never underestimate the helpfulness of the legislative assistant.
4. Be punctual, but calculate considerable waiting time in your agenda.
5. Have something in writing that concisely and clearly states your position or request and includes your name, address and phone number, along with that of your Association. Leave this with the Congressperson.
6. When making a series of personal calls, wear very comfortable shoes and an especially eye-catching hat, dress, or tie.

I was always a volunteer in the business of lobbying, so it took me many years to have the confidence to boldly proclaim my occupation as "lobbyist." By that time I had gained some credibility and was certain that lobbying was the best way to use my energy, no matter what organization or "cause" I was involved in.

I would never underestimate the need for well-qualified, highly motivated professional staff. They coordinate and direct the whole effort, provide needed research and keep a keen ear on any movements in legislative committees.

But volunteer advocates and lobbyists can be extremely valuable to a public interest campaign. As Margaret Mead said, "If you look closely, you will see that anything that embodies our deepest commitment to the way human life should be lived and cared for, depends on some form of volunteerism." Every successful social movement has relied on motivated volunteers.

But an impartial evaluation of these successful movements—civil rights, human rights, women's rights, children's rights, patients' rights, and more—would show two almost diametrically opposed conclusions: (1) They have made tremendous strides forward. (2) But there is so much yet to be done before we can speak too proudly of a nation that is the most wealthy, generous, and informed in the world.

Someone wrote about the construction of the pyramids: "No one was angry enough to speak out." We've devised the governmental and political mechanisms to make it easy for people to speak out. Yet many do not even vote. This apathy undermines our rights. And it makes it even more important for those of us who feel passionately about a cause to speak out.

The volunteers and staff persons I have worked with on public interest lobbying campaigns have been without exception highly motivated, well-informed, keenly sensitive, and, above all, enthusiastic about the cause. This is exactly what a democratic system desperately needs.

Why I Lobby in the Public Interest

by John Sparks
Vice President for Government Affairs
and Public Policy
American Symphony Orchestra League

Since I was six, I knew I wanted to be involved in politics. But as with most kids, the specifics of my future employment were a little hazy. Other than thinking about maybe being a high profile politician, people like me with a life-long interest in politics and government don't really know what they will do until they actually plop into the work world.

I never said I wanted to be a lobbyist of course. I didn't know what a lobbyist was, but I guessed it was a kind of specialized crook who wore good clothes and knew famous people in Washington. I *did* know that I wanted to be in politics. As soon as I grasped the concept of the nation-state, I was drawn to ideas about fairness and freedom, feeling for people who had been brutalized by governments less benign than our own.

I can remember two powerful images that pushed me down this path. One is pictures of black people being chased by police dogs and water from fire hoses in civil rights demonstrations in the South. The second is a magazine picture of a massacred family in a bathtub of blood in Cyprus.

Where I grew up, black people were about as rare as millionaires, but I could not fathom why they would be treated that way, especially in our own country. And I knew nothing about Cyprus or the history of ancient hatreds there, but I sensed how lucky we were to be in a country that, although quite flawed, had a history that promised that things could be better.

If you share this desire to make things better, public interest lobbying may be your slice of pie. My experience includes 13 years of grassroots issue organizing and Washington lobbying, 7-1/2 years of journalism and government service, and on-again, off-again involvement in political campaigns (that frequent graveyard of good intentions).

Being a charity lobbyist has been good work for me. Professionals in this field do not get rich, but we do not necessarily starve. And in a place such as Washington, DC, where most people spend their waking hours talking about work, thinking about work, and largely being defined by work, having work I really care about is crucial to personal sanity.

I didn't always do charity lobbying. For several years I had represented various clients—some for-profits, some governmental, some nonprofit. I carried our message to Congress and the Executive Branch, and also helped clients frame their messages for policymakers and the general public. The most deeply satisfying work I did was for an Indian tribe, when I not only sought more money for social needs on an economically depressed reservation, but I was also dealing with a centuries-old clash of cultures. This was great work, but it was in the context of a for-profit private firm (the Tribe was one client), which meant little control over the kinds of clients we had to represent. For some, I found the work less than galvanizing.

Some clients had such piddling objectives and concerns that, to attract attention, we had to make their problems/threats/achievements seem greater than they were. I was a bit morally bored: I didn't have a lust for widget promotion.

In 1992, I became a lobbyist for a specific charity field—America's 1,800 symphony and chamber orchestras. Lobbying for something I care about has been a tremendous source of satisfaction.

The past few years has been a very interesting time to be one of the country's handful of professional arts lobbyists. Thanks to controversies over "obscene" art, the National Endowment for the Arts had been transformed from a sleepy, rarely noted agency into the right-wing's favorite whipping boy. I found myself helping wage legislative war to protect federal funding for the arts, as well as dealing with tax policy and many other issues.

"The arts" were not the linchpin issue of my life, but there were some interesting underlying issues about culture, government, and *how we make laws*—the process of democracy, in other words. Plus, there was my interest in a really cool job (I mean, *the lobbyist for the nation's great orchestras*—how many people get to do that?). To many people, lobbying for music may sound like fun, but it doesn't exactly sound like saving humanity, either. But I have found great passion for this task, for two reasons. First is the importance of the arts to human creativity, which strongly relates to survival. The arts deal with one of our most basic, powerful needs: to express ourselves and find a common language.

The other reason I've found great passion for this work goes back to my interest in our political process. I believe in our democratic process: that it can make things better for people, as long as the process is not totally corrupted by demagoguery, distortion, and outright fiction. Which is precisely what I believed our opponents were doing, terribly distorting the work of the arts endowment, with terrible consequences for charities and artists. And some people were buying it. It can make you furious, frustrated, or depressed.

I got furious, which can be a useful thing. I can only work effectively if I feel passionate about what I do, while trying to retain a sense of balance and humor.

The key is not getting so frustrated or depressed that you withdraw from these battles. Public interest lobbyists are needed not only to fight for a good cause such as the arts, but also to fight to make the process of democracy work, refusing to allow demagoguery and distortion to win in the end.

Here is some of what I've learned about how to be effective:

- Remember that Congress, and probably your average state legislature, does generally function as intended: to represent the views of the majority, while observing some respect for minority rights. When you are on the losing side of an issue, this is hard to acknowledge; it will seem as though the politicians are a bunch of hooligans who can do no right. And there are plenty of elected officials with attitudes that can make nearly any citizen cringe. But democracy is inherently untidy and frequently disappointing, and this simple mantra has helped me bite my lip many a time when confronted by some absurdity: my cause has to live to fight another day, and a little discretion can help you in that next battle.

- Most legislators, even many of those who make me wonder how they ever got elected, want to do the right thing. Their definition of right can sometimes be pretty bizarre, but most of them will at least listen to legitimate information. Do not underestimate their capacity for learning something.

- Charities wear a presumptive white hat in public policy. That is good and can be useful. But beware the thin line between "white hat" and smug do-gooder. If you push a point of view too hard and allow the public or the legislator to get the idea that you think you are morally superior, you are in big trouble. Most people accept that we are lobbying for our vision of the public interest, but they want to feel free to disagree without being tagged as enemies of our noble cause.

- As comfortable as I am with talking (surprised?), as an advocate, I try to flip on a little listening switch. Doing so can help make me more persuasive over time. Some lobbyists are bad at listening, and it *is* hard to do when you must quietly listen to some freshly-minted legislative assistant spout nonsense for 10 minutes. But patiently listening helps you lay the groundwork for "requiring" them to listen to you. It can also help you understand how they think, which can lead to more effective language and arguments.

It is a challenge. But it is the struggle and self-discovery that make this work so stimulating, all in the service of a cause bigger than yourself. Not a bad way to make a living after all.

Why Public Interest Advocacy?

by Eden Fisher Durbin, Director,
Public Policy
YMCA of the USA

Some people have the heart and head for direct service. They have the extraordinary gift that enables them to sit through seemingly directionless discussions with temperamental teenagers, Head Start classes of noisy four-year-olds with runny noses, and General Equivalency Diploma (GED) courses where the multiplication table appears insurmountable. I do not share this gift. I learned rather quickly while working with abused pre-schoolers in Philadelphia that my strengths were working *on behalf of* children, not with them.

I grew impatient performing direct service. Yes, we taught Lyndell to talk in complete sentences and maintain eye contact, helped Missy refrain from eating her hair, and gave Hector the skills to cope with his chaotic household. But what about the other Lyndells and Hectors—the ones without the fortune of an intervention program? What about the flawed social service delivery system that allowed these vulnerable children to succumb to such abuse under the guise of "family preservation?" How could this system be fixed in order to prevent more Hectors?

I grew dissatisfied with the microcosm that Lyndell and Hector represented and became eager to get my arms around the bigger picture. I turned my attention away from the invaluable experience of front-line service delivery in Philadelphia to advocacy work at the YMCA of the USA. While absolutely nothing can improve without that direct

intervention at the individual level, advocacy allows one to make change that affects more than one person.

The impact of advocacy was not initially clear to me. I found myself preparing for days for a 20-minute meeting with a member of Congress to try to educate him or her on the critical issues facing youth. You have but a brief window to explain the child care crisis facing working families, the struggles facing single-parents, or the challenges facing inner-city youth. I would talk, cajole, and educate, but often it felt as if policymakers had limited time or interest in those I cared so deeply about— children and families. I understood that public interest advocacy was important— because it gives voice to those who do not have it. What I didn't understand was how long it sometimes takes for public interest advocacy to influence policy— and policymakers.

I came to understand the power of advocacy when Congress took on the issue of child care. YMCAs are the largest single provider of child care in the country, serving nearly half a million children every day. In 1989, the House version of what became the Child Care and Development Block Grant would have made public schools the only eligible recipient for federal school age child care funds. The YMCA of the USA put together a list of the many communities around the country that had chosen YMCAs—not the schools—to run school-based child care programs. Local YMCAs (and other community child care providers) urged their Representatives and Senators to support a more flexible approach. This information and advocacy enabled Senator Orrin Hatch (R-Utah) to lead a successful effort to prevent Congress from overriding local decisions and imposing a single, federally mandated approach to school-age child care.

But the need to advocate about how to spend federal child care funds was not over. Once the Child Care and Development Block Grant became law, more than $7 billion began to go to state governments, with few strings and little guidance. There was talk of limiting reimbursement rates, diverting funding from school-age care to pre-schools and lowering standards, all to make the dollars stretch. "Serve more kids" became the mantra in state capitols across the country. Very little thought was given to who would be served, how they would be served, and by whom.

YMCAs realized they could maintain their long-time focus on providing services and not get involved in the struggle to decide how this government money should be spent, but the dance of legislation would continue without them. Decisions about the use of this money would be made with or without their input—behind closed doors, at the eleventh hour by well-meaning but ill-informed lawmakers.

The YMCAs decided to expand their mission and adopt a new role in their communities: public interest advocates. They sat through hearings on funding distribution, positioned themselves as the primary providers of school-age care, and participated in local task forces charged with re-writing standards. Advocacy enabled the YMCA to expand beyond the reach of its programs. As a result, the movement became a leader on issues affecting youth and families.

As the YMCA experience makes clear, the power of public interest advocacy is extraordinary. Unfortunately, there are too few public interest advocates in Washington and fewer still in state capitals. There is room in advocacy for those like myself—with limited skills for direct service—*and* for those who want to balance their traditional role as service provider with the role of lobbyist. And while I would recommend public interest advocacy as a full-time profession, I am convinced that service providers are in an even better position to influence or inspire policy.

Advocates can help lawmakers marry the often-competing worlds of theory and practice. Providers—front-line workers—understand how to meet the needs of families. Their advice can help temper the ideological agendas of politicians. The result is more effective policies that successfully help those in need become contributing members of society. The result is better government.

To ensure the development of sound programs, service providers should share their knowledge and understanding beyond their staff, board, and contributors. They should join with those in Washington, in their state capital and on their city council in making the laws that affect those they are struggling to serve. What is learned from working with the Lyndell's and Hector's must be shared with policymakers. We know the needs of kids, families, and communities will continue to grow, so we must make sure the voices representing them also continue to grow.

Charity Lobbying in the Public Interest

by Dorothy A. Johnson, President and CEO Council of Michigan Foundations

Webster's defines a lobbyist as "a person, acting for a special interest group, who tries to influence the introduction of or voting on legislation or the decisions of government administrators." Except for the special interest part, this shoe fits. So, while I would not call myself a lobbyist, there is no question that I try, regularly, to influence government decision-making. In fact, I submit that those of us in the nonprofit sector are at great risk if we do not do so.

Our experience at the Council of Michigan Foundations (CMF) shows why involvement in the policy-making process is so important. The Council is a membership association of private, community, and corporate foundations as well as giving programs in Michigan. Our mission is to increase, enhance, and improve philanthropy and to assist grantmakers in effectively giving their money away. Advocacy has made CMF better able to accomplish this mission.

Michigan has a long and influential history of giving. This history involves some of the most well-known names in philanthropy, including Charles Stewart Mott, Margaret and Harry Towsley, Henry Ford, Herbert and Grace Dow, W.K. Kellogg, and Sebastian Kresge.

This philanthropic tradition continues: in 1996, more than 1,200 Michigan-based foundations gave away more than $800 million. Between 1994 and 1996, more than 150 new private foundations were created. And each of Michigan's 83 counties is served by a community foundation. CMF and our lobbying had a great deal to do with this success.

CMF was the principal advocate for a unique provision in Michigan law that provides an income tax credit to taxpayers making contributions to community foundations. Unlike the federal government, Michigan does not allow deductions for charitable giving. Michigan did, however, allow a tax credit—up to $200—for gifts to Michigan's state-run universities and public broadcasting stations. CMF saw this as a problem and an opportunity.

The problem was that there was no incentive for small givers to support other important institutions. Michigan's community foundations were doing great work. We wanted to enhance Michigan's rich history of individual giving by extending this credit to cover gifts to community foundations, a step that would help expand the reach and effectiveness of our state's community foundations. CMF members took the lead in advocating the credit, drafting the proposed statute, and bringing it to the attention of state officials, including the governor. Our proposal became law, with a Community Foundation Tax Credit line appearing on the annual Michigan income tax return.

More than any other factor, this tax credit has led to the expansion of our state's community foundations. Today, every Michigan resident is served by a community foundation, which they can choose to support as well as petition for assistance. Of all our advocacy activities in the past decade, I am most proud of this one. And it would not have happened had CMF not been willing to commit to the effort and had I not been willing to go to bat. You do not have to like the word "lobbying" to like the result of a good public policy, achieved through advocacy.

CMF's advocacy role is not new. Since 1977 we have sought legislation favorable to the creation and growth of private and community foundations, as well as corporate giving programs. To me it comes down to this question: if we do not speak for ourselves, who will? Charitable and philanthropic organizations need to speak out about government actions that affect us.

Because I believe Americans are the most generous people on earth, government has a responsibility to enhance philanthropy, not discourage it. In fact, government ought to be our strong ally: As welfare and entitlement programs are restructured, the burden on charities increases. Our work should have the respect and the assistance of government, not its suspicion. The best way to clear the air is to talk to each other. That means both parties, government and charity, need volunteers and staff who can talk each other's language.

To me, government relations is an educational undertaking. In whatever field in which we work—education, the arts, social well-being, the environment, philanthropy—we are the experts. We know more about our agencies and our work than outsiders. We can and should communicate this knowledge to those in government who take actions that affect us.

While few of us are professional lobbyists, we can still effectively communicate with those in government. We are their constituents. We elect them. Sometimes, as private citizens, we work as campaign volunteers, or contribute funds. Exercising our civic responsibility in this way is important for us all. New staff members ought to see civic activity as being part of their career, as it pays dividends for society as well as our agencies.

My recommendations are unambiguous. Charitable and philanthropic organizations need volunteers and staff who have the skill to work with government. (In our case, we hired a professional lobbying firm to give us advice.) Our organizations need to regularly exchange information on what we know about government activity. And when we agree about an issue, we need to work together.

Our organizations have the responsibility to communicate with government with the same level of expertise we bring to our philanthropic and service work. Those we serve deserve it. They count on us to do it well, and I know we can.

Being a Public Interest Lobbyist *Is* Something to Write Home About

by David Cohen, Co-Director
Advocacy Institute

David Cohen has been lobbying for the public interest for nearly four decades. He has fought for civil rights, voting rights, congressional reform, and campaign finance reform. He has fought against poverty, the Vietnam War, the MX Missile, and Star Wars. In 1985 he co-founded The Advocacy Institute, which works to strengthen the advocacy capacity of social justice organizations to set their public agenda.

If there is one person who can speak to the value of lobbying for the public interest—and who can tell us how to do it effectively—it is David Cohen. We think his reflections on what he has learned during his long and distinguished career are invaluable. He reflects on why he has devoted much of his public life to lobbying, how lobbying has changed, what these changes mean for public interest lobbyists, and what combination of values, skills, attitudes, and knowledge will make someone an effective public interest agenda setter.

Why I chose to be a lobbyist

I am a partisan of public interest lobbying. I have done it much of my professional life. Even when my job titles and descriptions changed, I worked at it. If a wrong can be repaired by lobbying, my juices flow.

Today many people disdain all lobbyists. But to me, being a public interest lobbyist is a career you can write home about and wear proudly at class reunions. My children knew I was a lobbyist. They were proud!

Such pride does not come from greater virtue or wisdom, nor does it come from enjoying life's luxuries. Being a public interest lobbyist can and should allow you to enjoy a decent life and raise a family, but you will not eat in posh restaurants, drive expensive cars, or fly first class.

No, I think the pride my children felt about my work came from the importance of what the public interest lobbyist does, combined with the attitudes, skills, and knowledge that an effective lobbyist develops.

The crucial roles of a public interest lobbyist

Most important, a public interest lobbyist helps create what social analysts call the "civic balance," allowing the public interest to be incorporated into public policy. A public interest lobbyist helps balance the many self interests that, naturally enough, push policy in ways that benefit narrow parts of the population. There's nothing inherently wrong with pursuing self interests. It has a legitimate voice in our process. Each of us has our own specific interests. But these self interests create a cacophony of special interests that must be balanced by people and groups that pursue the public interest.

By "public interest," I don't simply mean people pursuing causes in which I happen to believe. I don't agree with those who, in my view, are trying to dismantle our system for insuring health and safety and cut back on important public investments. But I do recognize that some of those fighting for these changes are motivated by what they believe is good for the public interest. I don't agree with them, but I do respect their commitment to their belief system.

Public interest lobbyists are especially concerned with incorporating the views of people who are not normally part of the process. Finding ways to organize and amplify, the voices of your members and constituents is one of the most satisfying—and challenging—aspects of being a public interest lobbyist. Seeing people who never participated in anything become engaged and empowering themselves—seeing their lives change—is extremely gratifying. That's why my colleagues and I see public interest advocacy as people-centered advocacy.

Indeed, the ability to generate sustained grassroots public participation has been one key distinction between public interest and special interest lobbying. This distinction has been blurred recently by various techniques that use money to distort the process. Special interests almost always have lots of money. The policies they pursue usually make a big financial difference for certain industries or individuals. So the money that special interests put into lobbying can easily be justified as an investment that may lead to a big payoff.

This simply isn't true for most public interest lobbying campaigns. We may believe that a certain policy change will have a big payoff for society as a whole. But such a change will seldom make a big, immediate difference in the bank accounts of a few rich people or industries, thus public interest lobbyists do not have access to big money.

As a result, we rely on broad public participation. Generating informed grassroots participation is a crucial role of a public interest lobbyist, and it can be one of the job's greatest satisfactions.

If you help generate this kind of participation, you can experience the greatest satisfaction of the public interest lobbyist: moving from "what is" to "what ought to be," carrying out the values you believe in and stand for. As I reflect on my lobbying career, it is the sense that I was part of some extraordinary changes— changes that have brought this country a little closer to what it "ought to be"—that makes me proud that I chose this career. But when we achieve an important change, we also know there are "no permanent victories." We have to be prepared to defend hard fought gains.

The important skills a good public interest lobbyist develops

While big changes are what we strive for, we can't rely on such successes to justify our decisions to be public interest lobbyists. Any policy can be reversed. Some policies take more than a lifetime to achieve. Some of my lobbying mentors worked for causes all their lives and never completed their work. They instinctively followed the values taught by the Talmud: Theirs was not to complete the task, but to start it and find ways to bring their visions alive, both in the minds of the public and policymakers. A good example is correcting the abuses of money in politics, an issue that people have struggled over for generations. With an issue like this, when progress can't be achieved in the short run through legislation, you do everything to keep the issue alive over time, educating and activating people so that, eventually, real change will come.

Fortunately, there are many benefits of a public interest lobbying career other than contributing to social change:

- Because the essence of lobbying is relationships (with constituents, policymakers, coalition partners, other staff members), you can learn much about how to relate to people, including those with whom you may not always agree.
- Similarly, being an effective lobbyist means learning how to be an effective team member. No one person can bring about an important policy change. You must learn to work with people both within and outside your organization.
- Being effective also means learning how to communicate with people outside your immediate world. If you are going to build broad public participation, you have to be able to do two things. You must learn to demystify the policy-making process, which allows people distant from that process to learn how to affect it—and to believe they *can* affect it. And you must learn to talk about your issue in ways that make it real and compelling to people who aren't immersed in

policy jargon. These are extremely valuable skills.

- In learning to communicate with a broad range of people, you learn to use modern methods of communication, including audio, video, and computers. These too are valuable skills.

How lobbying has changed, and what these changes mean for us

The need to learn about modern communication methods suggests some of the profound changes in the ways that policies are developed and the tools that lobbyists must use.

The image of a lobbyist used to be a cigar-chomping guy sitting in a bar with a legislator, trying to cut a deal. Over time that image evolved into a slicker looking guy wearing Gucci shoes, offering a legislator big bucks to give a speech at some Caribbean resort. No doubt there are still many lobbyists who smoke cigars and wear Gucci shoes—and legislators who find ways to get that expenses-paid trip to an island—but these images are misleading. The legislative process—and the ways it can be affected—have changed.

For one thing, lobbyists are no longer exclusively men. There are many women lobbyists, and not just those who advocate for issues like better child care. The head lobbyist of the National Rifle Association is a woman.

For another thing, the legislative process—especially in Washington—has changed radically. Whereas once a lobbyist could whisper in the ear of a few powerful legislators, now there are dozens of legislators who have power by sitting on or chairing one of the many committees and subcommittees that control legislation and oversee the bureaucracy. Plus, there are thousands of staff people who also wield power for these legislators and committees. And remember the invisible technicians and bureaucrats who write the rules that implement the laws.

The days of the lobbyist as sole practitioner have virtually ended. In the recent battle over protecting children's health from tobacco, the industry assigned an individual lobbyist to each senator. In the parlance of sports, this is person-to-person coverage!

Lobbying has changed big time, becoming a full-fledged industry with an estimated 35,000 lobbyists, in addition to researchers, public relations specialists, video producers, traditional organizers and the ubiquitous lawyers. These people surely number more than a 100,000. The lobbyists even have their own trade association.

The lobbying "industry" has grown so much mainly because, no matter which political party is in charge of Congress and the Executive Branch, the federal government remains the manager of the United States economy. Decisions it makes concerning spending, taxation, and regulations have enormous consequences—for individuals, industries, and the country as a whole. And not only do the government's decisions affect our pocketbooks, they also influence nearly every part of our lives—our education, health, environment, child care, the safety of our food and workplaces, and much more.

This is why so many people are trying to influence these decisions. They understand that Congress and the administration respond to those who are organized.

Indeed, the fact that the government will respond to organized, grassroots campaigns has led to one of the most important changes in lobbying. Increasingly, industries and others with big money are using modern technology to generate what appear to be large-scale, grassroots lobbying efforts. They will fax or e-mail lobbying messages to enormous numbers of people (the Chamber of Commerce, for example, has the names not only of every business that is a member, but each business's employees). Those people can respond by simply dialing a toll-free number, which will "patch" them directly to the office of their representatives or senators. Or, industries will finance expensive, sophisticated ad campaigns in key legislative districts, generating hundreds if not thousands of calls.

The messages these special interests communicate through their ads or directly through faxes and e-mail have been carefully honed to appeal to certain audiences, mainly by investing still more money in "focus groups" and opinion surveys that test and refine messages. In other words, what used to be the province of public interest lobbyists—grassroots response from people across the country—is now being widely used by special interest lobbyists. Thanks to low-cost technologies such as e-mail, faxes, and the Internet, all of this can happen very, very quickly, another major change in lobbying.

The need to work even harder at involving people in the process

These changes have big implications for public interest lobbyists. It has made it even more important for us to generate broad participation, while at the same time disclosing the "paid for" nature of the public participation generated by special interests.

To generate that broad participation, public interest lobbyists must see that their primary role is to make it possible for others to speak and act for themselves. At times, we may do what a traditional lobbyist does: advocate directly to legislators and staff members. But this kind of direct lobbying should be only a small part of the work.

To generate broad participation, we must work hard to make our issues clear to people, finding ways to get rid of the jargon that policymakers and lobbyists often use. We must frame the choices for our constituency, *not* make the decisions. A perfect example of what happens when the lobbyists make the decisions and don't involve enough people is catastrophic health insurance, a bill that was repealed shortly after it was passed even though President Reagan and the liberals supported it. The way catastrophic health care was funded alienated many people, people who hadn't been brought into the debate before the bill was passed.

In framing the choices, we must work particularly hard at educating people, trying to explain the policies that have led to the problems they are experiencing—with their schools, child care, neighborhoods, whatever. One key step in the long battle against toxins in our environment was the "right-to-know"

provision that was put into a piece of legislation. This provision required disclosure of information about toxins in every part of the country. Local people were trained to use this law, which allowed them to document their communities' problems. This in turn led to much broader public support for stronger environmental laws.

The need to explain the law-making process

To achieve broad participation, we must also make the process clear to people. The process of getting a law passed, especially on the federal level, can seem incomprehensible. Most people don't understand the difference between the Budget committee and Appropriations committees. They may not understand that, just because a bill has passed the House, it doesn't become law. They have no idea of the importance of a "conference committee" (which resolves differences between bills passed by the House and Senate). All most people see is lots of money being poured into lobbying battles and political campaigns, and many conclude that the average person has no power in this process.

Our role is to make clear the important role they can play. We need to be the "diagnostician," explaining what is happening, why, what *could* happen, and what people can do. Our role is not to "cut the deal," but to make sure that there are lots of informed lay people who know what's going on, why it's important, and whom to hold accountable. For example, on the tobacco bill that was stopped by some maneuvers in Congress in 1998, supporters understood that this crucial piece of legislation never even came up for a direct vote. They could then use this outrage to hold those who killed the bill accountable.

Indeed, pointing out outrages like this is another key role of the public interest lobbyist. To generate broad support, people need to care deeply about an issue. Not all issues can generate the kind of passion and commitment that leads to major changes, such as the civil rights movement and opposition to the Vietnam war. But most issues can be made compelling, especially if people see the large ideas that underlie the issue.

At the same time, the effective public interest lobbyist makes the concrete benefits of a policy clear: If this law passes, you will have the tools you need to get rid of toxins in *your* neighborhood.

The need to put it all together

Putting it all together—the big ideas and the concrete benefits—is another key role. Especially today, with the special interests devoting so much money to developing effective messages, we need to work hard at developing effective public arguments, ones that persuade people—particularly the unconvinced—to see the issue from a public interest perspective.

Effective public interest lobbyists must put it together in another way: They must be able to build strong relationships with a wide variety of people, both within and outside their organizations. Within the organization this includes members, organizers, media specialists, researchers, and support staff. Outside the organization this includes legislators and their staffs, journalists, and potential allies.

Public interest lobbyists rarely influence votes by themselves. We all dream of being the person who sways the deciding vote on some critical issue. But the chances of this happening are about as great as winning the lottery! Instead, the key is being part of a large team of people and organizations that together, over time, can change critical policies.

Especially in a public interest organization, where people are motivated by their commitment to a cause, lobbyists will fail if they exaggerate their importance and try to control the process. All they will accomplish is to alienate their most important asset: people who care enough to participate.

What attitudes make public interest lobbyists effective?

This commitment to being part of a team rather than a lone ranger is one of many attitudes that can help make a public interest lobbyist successful. These attitudes include:

- An internalized belief in democratic values and process.
- Accepting people for whom they are, regardless of race, religion, class, gender, disability, or credentials.
- A sense of possibility that changes can occur. An openness to trying new, sometimes bold, approaches.
- A willingness to challenge entrenched, institutionalized power, without being intimidated.
- A belief in people's capacity to do the job and follow through.
- Respect for other points of view, even those with whom you strongly disagree. By respecting other points of view, you don't make permanent enemies.

- Not personalizing disagreements, recognizing that allies sometimes disagree.
- Ability to express strong emotions such as love and anger in ways that strengthen rather than undermine the team effort.
- Respect and empathy for those you are trying to serve.
- Patience and restraint within your organization, recognizing that there are different roles for different people at different times.
- Stamina to engage in the usually long struggle to achieve—and maintain—significant changes.
- Openness with colleagues, which can allow for critical feedback that can strengthen rather than undermine the joint effort.
- The use of humor, which helps people keep perspective.
- The use of celebration, which helps pull people together, acknowledge their importance and maintain their commitment. You celebrate not just the occasional substantive victory—the new law you win—but also the more common "process" victory—the constructive meeting your members had with a legislator or editorial board member.
- Openness to innovation, which can lead to new techniques for lobbying, organizing, using information, building coalitions, and telling the story of your work.

This openness—combined with a willingness to seize the initiative—is critical. This is especially true today, when the special interests have adapted many public interest lobbying techniques. If we are to keep up, we must innovate.

I have seen the power of invention in each major issue in which I've been engaged. For example, in the 1960s before African-Americans gained the right to vote in the South, civil rights supporters adopted senators from states without a tradition of overt racial discrimination. This was a grassroots idea born and bred in the South. By educating these senators from states far removed from the harsh realities of the South, civil rights supporters gained enough support to make changes that went far beyond what most people at the time thought was possible.

Another example comes from the effort to end the Vietnam war. When powerful House chairmen refused to allow a vote on the issue, I helped invent the "Statement of Principles." With the support of key allies in the House of Representatives, this statement focused legislators on the simple position of ending the war by a certain date, cutting off funds for it, and bringing U.S. prisoners home. It led to a series of test votes on the issue, helping clarify the issues and building momentum for bringing an end to the Vietnam War.

What skills make public interest lobbyists effective?

Advocacy skills come over time, with experience, rather than through a formal credentialing process. But they only come if people are open to learning from their experiences, as well as from colleagues.

The underlying skill is similar to that of a family doctor or lawyer practitioner: someone who is a generalist, who has the ability to diagnose and prescribe remedies for a wide variety of situations. As with a good doctor or lawyer, one doesn't start with this ability. It comes over time, eventually becoming second nature. Specific skills include:

- The ability to listen to what your constituents, allies, and opponents are saying. A good doctor listens closely to a patient, not jumping to a diagnosis, listening for sometimes subtle clues. Every lobbying situation, like every patient or client, is a little different from what you have seen before.
- The ability to communicate effectively to members and the public. This can be harder than it seems. It is easy to fall into certain assumptions about an issue and how people will respond to it. It is easy to assume that everyone understands an issue and its importance as well as you and your colleagues understand it. Again, being able to listen closely to how people respond, to the questions they ask, is critical. If you find yourself isolated in a place like Washington, DC, the key is getting out as regularly as possible. It's too easy to be absorbed by the "insider" world, which can both limit your ability to communicate with people and rob you of your sense of what is possible.
- Being grounded in reality—in what is possible—while at the same time maintaining a vision of what you want and where you are heading. Being able to keep your eyes on the prize, in the words of the civil rights movement. I can name issue after issue—civil rights, the MX missile— where the conventional wisdom (that the MX missile was a done deal, for example) turned out to be completely wrong.

- The ability to write and edit quickly. While the legislative process can move painfully slowly, there are often constant small steps and changes that require analysis and response. The ability to produce quick drafts is very useful.
- The ability to analyze and synthesize diverse and complex material.
- The ability to motivate others by telling stories, using humor and drama, and building strong teams.
- The ability to negotiate, mediate, and drive a hard bargain. This requires adapting to different situations, being realistic about your opponents and allies.
- The ability to build strong personal and public relationships that can survive disagreements and allow you to work with former adversaries.

Don't let this long list of skills discourage you. One reason working with others and building a team is so important is that different people and organizations bring different skills. You may be a great negotiator. Someone else may be a great writer. Another person may be a superb strategist. You need a range of skills, but you don't need to be great at every skill.

What knowledge makes public interest lobbyists effective?

There are two types of knowledge that good lobbyists need. One is simply knowing the basic tools of the trade: how to identify possible allies on an issue, how to work with a coalition, how to set up a meeting with a legislator or staff member, which people should meet with the legislator and what should be said, how to summarize an issue into a few, cogent "talking points," how to testify at a legislative hearing, and much more.

The other type of knowledge is less concrete. As with skills, this type of knowledge comes from experience. It involves things like the interaction between the formal and informal rules and procedures of a legislative body. You need to know the rules and procedures of the legislative body you are trying to influence. Equally important is knowing the answers to questions such as: How does the formal structure mesh with the informal practice? Who actually makes decisions? What procedures must they follow? To whom does the decision-maker listen? Who will take public responsibility? Are there budgetary or legal restraints?

You also need to know as much as you can about external factors that could influence decision-makers. How sensitive are decision-makers to public pressure, media attention or embarrassment? Are there certain people or groups to whom a decision-maker must be particularly sensitive for political reasons? Has there been a recent event that may sway a decision, such as a child killed by a drunk driver or a teenager killed by a handgun?

I gained this type of knowledge not by reading but by observing and talking with lots of people. This type of knowledge usually can't be found in guidebooks.

If this isn't enough, many decisions today are affected by larger forces. Decisions by a state government are often affected by the rules or direction of the federal government. Decisions of the federal government can be affected by

international concerns. This is particularly true for economic, trade, and environmental issues.

Given all this complexity, you also need to know how to help your organization forge a realistic strategy. What are your potential advantages and strengths? Challenges and weaknesses? What factors could undermine your goal? What ties do you have to individuals or groups that can be helpful? What's the best way to frame the issue and generate public support?

Concluding thoughts

The task of creating change can easily seem daunting, and it is for one person or one organization. You must have allies, including those with whom you may not always agree. And you must keep in mind that you are engaged in a long-term process, one that involves building broader public participation in decision-making as well as building more relationships with those who can influence policy decisions.

You may well lose in the short-term, but the key is what happens over time, both in relation to specific policies and in how people and policymakers think about your issues. We had over a dozen votes before Congress was convinced to vote to stop funding the Vietnam War. But over time we were able to erode support for the war by changing people's perceptions of it, getting them to focus on its enormous cost in lives and dollars.

Even if you win in the short-term, there are no permanent victories in this work. As Yogi Berra put it, "The game isn't over until it is over." The reality is, the game is never over. I've been working on campaign finance reform for more than 30 years. We have won some victories. But we are obviously still a long way from gaining the comprehensive institutionalized changes necessary to end the corrupting effect of money in politics. The same is true of civil rights and the social safety net: Laws that once seemed permanent face threats. Which is why you have to be in public interest lobbying for the long haul, celebrating victories but not being lured to sleep by them, learning from defeats but not being overwhelmed by them.

What it all adds up to is that the public interest lobbyist must be prophetic and priestly. The prophet is the visionary, helping us see what could exist, recognizing that we must move past ourselves, that we cannot be only for me, as the sage Hillel pointedly reminds us.

Similarly the public interest lobbyist draws out the ideas that can energize people and keep them involved for the long-term struggle that real change always requires.

The priest helps people keep their faith. Similarly, the public interest lobbyist must keep alive the belief and faith that our democratic political system will respond to those who participate in it, that it will reach out to those who have been historically excluded. It doesn't always pass this test. But it has passed it often enough to make it continuously worth testing. Think about the many fundamental changes our system has experienced over time, from voting rights for minorities and women to a safety net for seniors.

This strategy of change through broad participation diminishes the fantasy of leader-rescuers: the idea that a president or a charismatic leader will make the changes we think are needed. Today in a democracy, a leader can only act if the path has already been laid out, by citizens who have been effectively pushing for changes over many years.

This strategy, by emphasizing the need to inform and involve people beyond Washington's Beltway, also diminishes the importance of the "inside" experts with their narrow technical fixes. Certainly a technical change in a regulation can make a difference. But those working for the public interest must keep the long-term focus on the major changes that will really improve the lives of many people, changes that can only happen as a result of widespread participation and understanding.

Just as the religious leader keeps the group's focus on its mission, so the public interest lobbyist must keep the group's focus on its mission. That can only be achieved when the group organizes, educates, engages and involves large numbers of people.

The challenge is to blend the prophetic vision with the priestly attributes of faith and attention to the mundane and ordinary—the day to day work of building an organization, strengthening a coalition, making room for new leaders, nurturing public and personal relationships, doing the research and raising the money. We need it all. Each reinforces the other, helping make real and lasting improvements in people's lives, insuring that their voices will be heard and their concerns become the public agenda.

Resource A

Questions from Real-Life Examples Regarding Activities Related to Lobbying and Voter Education by Nonprofits

Nonprofit organizations often have asked INDEPENDENT SECTOR whether certain activities are lobbying under the 1976 lobby law. Questions also have been raised regarding what voter education activities are permissible during a political campaign. Following are examples of the kinds of questions asked, with answers, and the page where you can get more information:

Is it lobbying?

1. Issue

A mental health association has a position in support of legislation to provide a range of community services for homeless persons who are mentally ill. It provided information on the legislation, and the association's support for it, in the association's legislative alert to its members, as well as in its Annual Report and several other documents sent to its members. The information did not include a request that the readers of the publications contact their legislators in support of the legislation, nor did it give any legislator's name and address or provide a tear off petition to be mailed to a legislator.

Answer

The activity is not lobbying. The organization can refer to legislation, including the group's position on it, in its communication *to its members*, and that activity does not constitute lobbying, so long as the association does not ask its members to contact legislators in support of the measure, (p. 53) or give any legislator's name and address or provide a tear off petition to be mailed to a legislator.

2. Issue

The same mental health group mentioned above provided information on the legislation and its position on it in a letter to members of the state legislature. The letter did not ask the legislators to support the legislation.

Answer

The activity is lobbying. By mentioning the legislation to legislators and the organization's position on it, the mental health group engaged in lobbying, (p. 56).

3. Issue

An environmental organization focusing on safe drinking water was invited in writing by a committee of Congress to testify on legislation being considered by the Committee. The group's Board Chairperson testified and stated opposition to the legislation, maintaining that the measure would weaken the current law safeguarding drinking water.

Answer

The testimony was not lobbying because the *Committee* had invited the group in writing to testify. If the organization had requested to testify, or had been asked to testify by a *single legislator* instead of the Committee, the testimony would have been lobbying, (p. 53).

4. Issue

An association providing disaster relief conducts exhaustive nonpartisan research on methods to respond more rapidly and effectively when disaster strikes. The research concludes that disaster relief legislation currently being considered by the state assembly should be supported. The organization distributed the research broadly to its members and makes it available to the public. The research includes a full and fair exposition of the pertinent facts to permit the audience to form an independent opinion.

Answer

The research is not considered a lobbying expenditure even through it takes a position in support of the disaster relief legislation. The fact that the association's research included a *full and fair exposition of the facts*, made the material generally available, and *did not include a direct call for the readers to take action*, provides the basis for the research to be considered a non-lobbying expenditure, (p. 54).

5. Issue

An education association that receives federal funds sends a letter to all members of Congress opposing legislation that would curtail the lobbying rights of nonprofits that receive federal funds.

Answer

The letter is not a lobbying expenditure because it is a "self-defense" activity. Lobbying legislators (but not the general public) *on matters that may affect the organization's own existence, powers, tax exempt status, or the deduction of charitable contributions to it*, do not count as direct lobbying expenditures. However, had the education association taken an *ad in the newspaper* calling on readers to oppose the legislation it would count as a lobbying expenditure. While self-defense lobbying activities do not count as direct lobbying expenditures, that exception does not extend to grassroots legislative activities such as the newspaper ad, (p. 53).

6. Issue

Volunteers with a statewide arts organization urge the organization's members from throughout the state to march on the capitol in support of arts funding. Four hundred members spend two days, at their own expense, meeting with legislators and the governor. Members planned and conducted the march, and used their own funds for promotional materials, getting the word out on the march, briefing sheets and all other activities related to the march. The arts organization spent no money on the march.

Answer

The march is not lobbying. Lobbying takes place *only when there is an expenditure of a nonprofit's money* on an activity that constitutes lobbying, (p. 53). If the arts organization had spent any funds urging its members to participate in our march, those amounts would have been considered lobbying expenditures.

Is it permissible activity during a political campaign?

1. Issue

The Board Chairperson of an association that provides family services is invited to a fundraiser for the mayor. The Chairperson makes a personal contribution to the mayor's campaign, urges the mayor to support child welfare legislation under consideration by the city council, mentions that she is Chairperson of the family service association but states that she is speaking as a private citizen, not as a representative of the family service association.

Answer

The activity will not be attributed to the organization because she gave a *personal* check as a campaign contribution and made clear she was speaking as a *private* citizen, not as a board member of the family services association. Nor was the statement in support of the legislation lobbying by the association because the Chairperson said she was *speaking as a private citizen*, (p. 66).

2. Issue

A disabilities group is conducting a bike-a-thon fundraiser during a local election for city council. At the start of the event, a candidate for city council shows up, unannounced, wanting to participate in the bike-a-thon, make a brief two minute campaign statement, and pass out campaign literature.

Answer

The city council candidate can participate in the bike-a-thon as a *private citizen*, but not as a candidate for public office and cannot make a statement or pass out campaign literature.

3. Issue

A statewide health organization typically holds its annual meeting in January, at the state capitol. This year, the organization wants to present an award to a state senator who recently spearheaded the enactment of legislation strongly supported by the health organization.

Answer

The organization may present the award if the presentation does not occur during an election campaign.

4. Issue

The Board Chairperson of a women's rights organization has decided to run for the state legislature. Can she continue to serve as Chairperson of the organization?

Answer

She can continue to serve as Chairperson of the organization but should be certain not to use her position as Chairperson to provide a platform for her campaign or to in any way suggest that the organization has a position on her candidacy, (p. 66).

5. Issue

A disaster relief organization sends a survey to candidates for the state legislature asking their position on increased appropriations for disaster relief services. The organization does not plan to release the survey information until after the election.

Answer

The organization may send the survey to the candidates, but by not releasing the survey results until after the election, it has not engaged in partisan political activity.

Resource B

Lobbying by Nonprofits: A Checklist

Lobbying isn't a very complicated process. If you can pick up a pen or a phone, you can lobby. This checklist will help you skim quickly through the main subjects covered by this book and know what will be most helpful to you. While you are skimming, keep in mind that most how-to books, including this one, tell you much more than you'll ever need to know about how to get the job done.

You Need to Know Only a *Little* About the Following to Get Started Lobbying (Chapter 1)

1. The legislative process
2. Organizing your group's government relations committee
3. Setting up a legislative network
4. The law governing lobbying by nonprofits

The Nonprofit Lobbyist's Skills and the Legislative Process (Chapter 2)

1. You don't need a paid lobbyist—a volunteer lobbyist can do the job.
2. What your lobbyist needs and needs to know
   - A few basics about the legislative process
   - Several main arguments for the bill you are supporting
   - Your group's organizational structure and how it communicates with its grassroots.
3. Strong interpersonal skills

Selecting Your Leader in the Legislature (Chapter 2)

1. You'll need a strong advocate for your bill in the legislative committee that has jurisdiction over your legislation
2. Skills and commitment of the legislative staff person assigned to your measure are often crucial to success.

The Legislative Process (Chapter 2)

1. The legislative process is controlled by people, not by institutions.
2. In both chambers of a legislature, legislation usually moves from subcommittee to full committee to a floor vote, and then to conference between the two chambers. At each step of the process, it is possible to influence the outcome of the legislation, but the best chance is at the subcommittee level.
3. All members of a legislature are not equal. Majority party members have more power than minority members. Senior members are usually more influential than newer members.

4. The legislative process is run by people. Put yourself in your legislator's shoes.
5. Don't take a legislator's vote against your proposal personally. Maybe the legislator will be with you next time.
6. Staff people are important. Senior staff people may wield enormous power. They can assist you greatly in guiding your legislation to enactment.

Lobbying the Administration (Chapter 2)

1. Your group's success in enacting legislation can be lost through restrictive regulations.
2. Nonprofits often have modest influence on the executive branch when lobbying them directly, but the executive branch can be moved with the aid of legislators.
3. Media support for your position, and criticism in the media of the government's position, can have an enormous impact.

Effective Communications (Chapter 3)

1. Be *accurate*. You, your legislator, and your cause all lose from the fallout of inaccurate information.
2. Be *brief*. Almost no one wants to read more than one page.
3. Be *clear*. Even those who are new to your subject shouldn't have to struggle to understand your communication.
4. Be *timely*. Your communication must arrive with sufficient lead time for grassroots recipients to contact legislators before a vote.
5. Follow up with a telephone call. Most people don't respond to written communications without a follow-up call.
6. Be familiar with new communications technologies.

Highly Effective Lobbying Techniques and Communications (Chapter 4)

1. Spontaneous letters from constituents
2. Personal visits by constituents
3. Articles in state/district newspapers
4. Telephone calls from opinion leaders in the state/district
5. Congressional Research Service
6. Telephone calls from constituents

Letters to Legislators (Chapter 4)

1. Write on your personal or business letterhead.
2. Keep your letter to one page, and put your message in your own words.
3. Ask the legislator to reply, and ask very directly whether he or she will support your position.
4. Like everyone else, legislators don't like a threatening tone.
5. Don't overstate your organization's influence.
6. Be certain that your legislator receives your letter before the vote.
7. Thank the legislator.

Meeting with Your Legislator (Chapter 4)

1. You may be nervous, but remember that you probably know more about the subject than the legislator does.
2. Make an appointment.
3. It's acceptable to bring a small delegation.
4. Discuss your issue from the legislator's perspective.
5. If you can't answer a question, don't bluff.
6. Leave a fact sheet.
7. Write to say thanks and to remind the legislator of agreements reached.

Presenting Testimony (Chapter 4)

1. Keep your statement brief, and provide a one-page summary.
2. A high-ranking, well-informed volunteer should be the presenter. A senior staff member is a second choice.
3. Get other groups to sign your testimony.
4. Plant questions with friendly legislators.
5. Oral statements should not be read.
6. It's perfectly acceptable to be direct in your response to a hostile question, but be courteous.
7. If you can't answer a question, say so, and offer to get the information.

Telephoning Your Legislator Regarding a Vote (Chapter 4)

1. If you can get through, a telephone call can be very persuasive.
2. Keep your call brief.
3. If you can't get through to the legislator, ask for the aide assigned to the issue.
4. If you can't reach the aide, leave your message with the person who answered the phone.
5. Calls to the district office of a legislator are second best but much better than nothing.

Other Ways to Communicate with Legislators (Chapter 4)

1. Invite them to visit your facility.
2. Have legislators speak at a public meeting sponsored by your organization.
3. Invite legislators to meet with your board of directors.
4. Sponsor a breakfast meeting at the Capitol.

Grassroots Action Through a Legislative Network (Chapter 5)

1. A grassroots network is an organized, systematic means of communicating on short notice with volunteers at the local level who have agreed to contact their legislators on behalf of your issue.
2. Grassroots networks don't have to be elaborate.
3. Volunteers are more influential with legislators than nonprofit staff are.
4. Setting up a network:
   - Get a list of legislators you want to contact.
   - Recruit volunteers who can establish contact with those legislators.
   - Develop a means of communicating very quickly with members of your network, including telephone calls.
   - Work at it. Networks are absolutely essential, but they atrophy quickly if you do not give them top priority.

Lobbying in Coalition (Chapter 6)

1. Almost all major legislation is enacted as a result of a coalition's efforts.
2. Coalitions are always fragile but have a potentially enormous influence over legislation.
3. A main function of coalition leaders is to build a sense of trust and openness, with honesty and "no surprises" paramount.
4. Every coalition must have an organization that serves as a clearinghouse.
5. The clearinghouse function—getting information to coalition members quickly—is critically important.
6. Coalition membership may change markedly over time, depending on other issues important to some of your coalition's members.
7. In coalition action, it can take as many as four steps in the process to get information from the coalition to the person being asked to take action at the grassroots, so plan carefully.
8. When a coalition effort is successful, make certain that all members are aware of the important role they played in the success.

Key Points About a Government Relations Committee (Chapter 7)

1. The biggest mistake made by government relations committees of nonprofits is to take on more than one top priority.
2. The committee can have 20 issues on its priority list, but all must be ranked.
3. A committee member may push the staff hard to emphasize his or her pet priority, even though the committee has decided otherwise. Don't give in.
4. The committee should delegate authority to a small group for decisions on legislation when time doesn't permit consultation with the parent group.
5. The committee should broadly represent the organization's constituency.
6. According to the size of the organization, much of the government relations committee's work should be delegated to task forces or other subgroups.
7. At meetings, pay attention to process:
   - Agendas are important.
   - Set a cordial tone.
   - Pay attention to the physical arrangements of the table and the meeting room.
   - Don't let the chair, the staff, or anyone else dominate.
   - Save everyone embarrassment by using name tent cards at each place.

Lobbying Through the Media (Chapter 8)

1. Legislators take note of organizations that the media quote in news stories on key legislative issues.
2. Congressional staff rank news articles and editorials in state/district newspapers very high as forces that influence members of Congress.
3. A person with experience in media relations (he or she may be a volunteer) can save your group much time by helping you target your media efforts.
4. Points to keep in mind:
   - Send only newsworthy information to the media.
   - There is a herd instinct in the media, which can help your media campaign snowball if you get one story in the influential media.
   - Reporters look for quotable sources. Have your off-the-cuff remarks well rehearsed.
   - Keep a list of media people who have contacted you or written or spoken on your issue—they represent a future resource gold miner

- A press release should give the most important information in the first paragraph, and the rest in descending order of importance. The first page of the release should answer *who, what, when, where,* and *why.*

5. Press conferences:
   - In most major metropolitan areas, it is difficult to get good press conference attendance because there are always so many competing issues.
   - Know the hour and day that the press are most likely to attend.
   - Know the location that will attract reporters.
   - Know how far in advance the press must be notified and how best to do so.
   - Give a reminder call on the day of the press conference.
   - Have a well-written press statement and background.
   - Be certain that your audio system is flawless.
   - Keep it short, and leave time for questions.
   - Keep a list of attendees for follow-up.

6. Letters to the editor:
   - Keep the letter tightly composed.
   - Use specific examples.
   - Address one point per letter.
   - Use accurate, up-to-date information.
   - Don't attack the opposition.
   - Always sign your name, and include your address and telephone number.

7. Radio and television:
   - Radio and television still offer public service time.
   - Don't forget news directors of radio and television stations when circulating your press release.
   - It helps greatly to have a visual angle for your television news story.
   - Keep your public service spots short: for TV, nine to ten seconds; for radio, twenty to thirty seconds.
   - Get a well-briefed spokesperson for your group on a radio or television talk show.
   - Give local radio or television your ideas for editorials.

Resource C

Questions and Answers

Regarding the Law and Lobbying by Nonprofits (Chapter 9)

1. Q: Is lobbying legal?

A: It's not only legal but also encouraged by Congress and the IRS.

2. Q: How much can I spend on lobbying?

A: A generous amount: 20 percent of your organization's first $500,000 of annual expenditures, 15 percent of next $500,000, 10 percent of the next $500,000, and so on, up to $1 million.

3. Q: Can all nonprofits spend that much?

A: No, only those that elect.

4. Q: Elect what?

A: Elect to come under the generous provisions of the 1976 lobby law.

5. Q: How do I elect?

A: It's simple. Have your organization's governing body vote to come under the 1976 law and file IRS form 5768.

6. Q: Will the IRS "red flag" us for audit if we elect the lobby law?

A: Absolutely not. The IRS has made that clear.

7. Q: That's all there is to it?

A: Yes. Sign IRS form 5768, and send it to the IRS.

The "Insubstantial" Rule (Chapter 9)

1. Q: What if we don't elect?

A: You are subject to the vague "insubstantial" rule.

2. Q: What does the "insubstantial rule" mean?

A: If you engage in "more than insubstantial" lobbying, you lose the right to receive tax-deductible contributions and lose your exemption.

3. Q: What is "more than insubstantial"?

A: That's not clear. Several court decisions have addressed the definitions.

4. Q: What did the courts find?

A: In 1955, that 5 percent of total activities is not substantial; in 1974, that each case must be evaluated according to "facts and circumstances"; and in 1972, that a percentage test is inappropriate, since a single official position statement could be considered substantial.

5. Q: How can I avoid this confusion?

A: Elect to come under the 1976 lobby law.

What Is Lobbying Under the 1976 Lobby Law? (Chapter 9)

1. Q: If I elect to come under the 1976 lobby law, which of my activities will be lobbying?

A: Any attempt to influence any legislation through communication with any member or employee of a legislative body or with any government official or employee who may participate in the formulation of the legislation (called *direct lobbying*), and any attempt to influence any legislation through an attempt to affect the opinions of the general public or any segment thereof (called *grassroots lobbying*).

2. Q: Can you make that less confusing?

A: Maybe. Direct lobbying occurs when a nonprofit organization (including its members who reside at the grassroots) contacts a policymaker on behalf of legislation. You are doing direct lobbying in your communications only if you refer to specific legislation and reflect a view of its merits. Grassroots lobbying occurs when a nonprofit organization contacts the general public and urges people to contact policymakers in support of legislation. You are doing grassroots *lobbying* if, in communicating with the general public, you refer to specific legislation, reflect a view of its merits, and encourage the general public to contact legislators.

3. Q: May I spend all of my total allowable lobbying expenditures on grassroots lobbying?

A: No. Only 25 percent may be spent on grassroots lobbying.

4. Q: Is there a similar limitation on direct lobbying?

A: No. You may spend 100 percent of allowable expenditures on direct lobbying.

5. Q: How do the new IRS regulations affect lobbying?

A: They provide helpful details regarding what is and is not treated as direct and grassroots lobbying.

6. Q: What are some other key issues covered by the lobbying regulations?

A: For grassroots lobbying, there is a special rule for paid mass-media messages. The regulations also define when materials developed in the previous six months and used in lobbying are a lobbying expenditure. They also explain how to allocate the costs of a communication that includes both a lobbying and a nonlobbying expenditure. They make clear when nonpartisan analysis study or research is not a lobbying expenditure.

7. Q: Is that all I need to know about the regulations?

A: It depends. If you plan to do what you consider extensive lobbying, you should read Chapter 9. If your lobbying is limited, simply keep in mind that the lobbying latitude under the law is generous.

Other Lobbying Limits (Chapter 10)

1. Q: What is self-defense lobbying?

A: Lobbying on legislation affecting the existence of the organization itself, its powers and duties, its tax-exempt status, or the deductibility of contributions to it.

2. Q: What are the limits on self-defense lobbying?

A: There are no limits on self-defense direct lobbying. Grassroots lobbying isn't protected by the self-defense provision.

3. Q: What are examples of self-defense lobbying?

A: Lobbying in support of charitable-contribution tax deductions or to change the law regarding lobbying rights of nonprofits.

Voter Education by Nonprofits (Chapter 10)

1. Q: May nonprofits carry out voter education during a political campaign?

A: Yes, if it is strictly nonpartisan.

2. Q: What kind of voter education is legal?

A: It's legal to inform candidates of your position. If the candidate goes on record on your issue, the candidate may distribute the statement, but you may not. You may distribute the answers to a nonpartisan questionnaire and hold nonpartisan forums.

3. Q: What about questionnaires to candidates?

A: A nonprofit can disseminate responses from questionnaires, but the questions must cover a broad range of concerns, be framed without bias, and be given to all the candidates for an office.

4. Q: What about distributing voting records of candidates?

A: You may, if you distribute voting records throughout the year and not just during the campaign.

5. Q: May I invite candidates to a public forum to get their views?

A: Yes, if you invite all candidates, are evenhanded, don't state your views or comment on candidates' views; and give all candidates the opportunity to answer questions.

6. Q: May I publish information from the forum?

A: Yes, in your newsletter, if it is published regularly, and if its circulation is limited to your organization's members. Candidates should also be given equal opportunity to reply.

Foundations and Nonprofits' Lobbying (Chapter 10)

1. Q: May nonprofits use private foundation grants to lobby?

A: Private foundation grants that are awarded for general purposes may be used by nonprofits to lobby, but funds earmarked for lobbying may not be used.

2. Q: May nonprofits use community foundation grants to lobby?

A: Nonprofits may receive grants from community foundations that *are* earmarked for lobbying.

Other Issues (Chapter 10)

1. Q: Is urging voters to put a proposal (an initiative)
on a ballot lobbying?

A: Yes, it's direct lobbying.

2. Q: Is urging members of a legislature to put a
law passed by the legislature (referendum) on the
ballot lobbying?

A: Yes, it's direct lobbying.

3. Q: Can a Section 501(c)(3) organization lobby
indirectly through a 501(c)(4) organization?

A: Yes.

4. Q: Why consider such an arrangement?

A: A 501(c)(4) organization may spend all of its funds on lobbying—
but contributions to it aren't tax-deductible.

5. Q: Are there any cautions regarding such an
arrangement?

A: Keep good records that show clearly how staff time, equipment,
office space, costs, and so on, are divided between the groups, and
be sure the (c)(3) doesn't provide financial support to the (c)(4).

6. Q: May a 501(c)(3) organization set up a political action
committee (PAC)?

A: No.

7. Q: May a 501(c)(4) set up a PAC?

A: Yes.

8. Q: May nonprofits use federal funds to lobby?

A: No, with the exception of lobbying specifically authorized by
federal law.

9. Q: May nonprofits use federal funds to provide technical
assistance?

A: Yes, if requested to do so by legislators.

10. Q: May they use federal funds for self-defense lobbying?

A: Yes—for example, to avoid material impairment of the organization's authority to perform with respect to a grant, a contract, or an agreement.

11. Q: How are lobbying expenditures reported to the IRS?

A: On IRS Form 990A Schedule.

12. Q: Must nonprofits that don't elect to come under the 1976 law report lobbying expenditures to the IRS?

A: Yes.

How to Win the Advocacy Game:
Rarified Air, by Doug Siglin

*"You can lead these horses to water, but
it's a lot harder to make 'em pass legislation,"
reports Doug's favorite hill staffer.*

I've been thinking a lot about trying to explain this business of successful issue advocacy with Congress.

Last night, as I watched my college alma mater play basketball on TV, a simple idea came to me. Although sports analogies are usually too facile to be of much real use, I'm going to put this one out for your consideration.

Here it is: Successful basketball teams have to be able to play both a good *inside* and a good *outside* game. So do groups that are consistently successful at working with Congress.

In basketball, the inside game is generally the purview of the centers and forwards. They block off the middle of the court, reject opposing shots, get rebounds, and make the high percentage of field goals from under the basket. The outside game generally belongs to the guards. They pressure the other team, direct the offense, and make those 15-20 foot jumpers look easy. A team that doesn't have both good inside and good outside games may win, but it won't be consistently good.

In the congressional case, there is also an inside game and an outside game. The inside game is building trusting relationships, learning how the situation looks from those most intimate with it, and getting voluntary help. The outside game is "pressuring" members of Congress. The two must go together in order to win consistently.

The Inside Game

Despite the general impression to the contrary, being a member of Congress is an outrageously tough job. Most members are on the go six or seven days a week from sunrise to long past sunset.

- They are continually being asked to do things for people they barely know or don't know at all.
- They have groups of constituents to meet in their offices or take to the Capitol steps for pictures.
- They have dozens of joint committees, standing committees, select committees, subcommittees, state delegation, special caucus, and task force meetings to attend, usually simultaneously.

- They have to stay awake and look interested through boring technical hearings on arcane matters.

Moreover, they have to continually deal with the press and be prepared to dispense witty new pearls of wisdom to groups during breakfasts, lunches, and dinners. They have to answer letters, make military academy nominations, write dozens of recommendation letters, battle with federal agencies, and fly back to their districts as often as they can hack it. They have to manage dual, triple, or quadruple offices and staffs, two residences, and their own families. They have to mind their political P's and Q's or they will find themselves jobless. And perhaps most annoying, they have to withstand constant abuse and have to be perpetually vigilant about what they say, even at their tiredest, crankiest moments. Just in terms of the energy it takes to be a member of Congress, these people are heroes.

When asked to take a position or some action on any given issue, a member of Congress will probably base a decision on a mix of at least six factors: (1) who is asking; (2) what they personally want to do; (3) what is good for the people they represent; (4) what is good national policy; (5) what is politically realistic; and (6) what won't get them rudely unselected. Staff have to make similar sorts of judgments, taking all these things into consideration on behalf of their bosses, plus some other factors of their own, like their positions in the office and how much the boss delegates.

Being human, members of Congress and staff are far more inclined to try to work with people over time who are more than just a letter or a phone call—particularly people who understand the other five parts of the mix and tailor their requests accordingly. They are likely to give such people the straightforward information that is such a valuable commodity. And if the member of Congress one has built a trusting relationship with is a committee chair or has some other high-ranking position, important doors can be opened with a very few words.

The bottom line on the inside game is this: if you establish honest relationships with members of Congress and their staffs and respect the limitations they face, they'll be far more inclined to *voluntarily* give you a hand.

The Outside Game

The outside game is the pressure individuals and groups can put on members of Congress to somewhat less voluntarily do what is wanted.

The pressure game comes in many forms, but in the end it comes down to this: making members of Congress fear that they won't get reelected. Members of Congress almost always want to get reelected (and more than 95 percent of them do). They often begin thinking about the next election well before the current one is wrapped up.

There is a lot of attention today about the role of money in politics, but the question of money is almost always ultimately a question of votes. Campaigns have become fantastically expensive—it's said that the average senator has to raise $10,000 dollars every working day to get reelected. Money equals TV time and billboards and yard signs and rallies and photo opportunities, and those equal votes. Groups that have lots of cash can play a great outside game.

But even those who don't have money can play a pressure game. The hunger lobbying groups RESULTS has figured out a wonderful way to do this. It gets its supporters to convince local newspaper editorial boards to write editorials about hunger, and then it sends reams of them to members of Congress. It's a wonderful and original pressure technique, and it has been quite effective. Other pressure techniques are letters…postcards, citizen press events and rallies, newspaper advertisements, and the like.

These outside game techniques get the attention of members of Congress, and if large or impressive enough can make them fear for their careers— and subsequently pay far more attention to the issues driving the pressure.

Last week's pay raise fiasco was a unique but interesting example of pressure. I don't think many lessons can be drawn from the case because of the intense public outrage at a 51 percent pay increase in a time of budget cuts, but do you know what eventually made the House change its collective mind? Tens of thousands of *tea bags!*

Here's what I think the point of all this is: both the inside game and the outside game are critical. Members will often respond to pressure techniques—particularly members who are less "safe" in their seats—but they do so unwillingly. Moreover, the "movers and shakers" have safe seats or they wouldn't be where they are. There are practical limitations to what pressure can do.

On the other hand, the *inside game* depends on an ability to establish a trusting relationship with members or their staffs: something which is often critical in the case of key individuals but isn't practical for all 538 members of Congress. This is also a limitation.

Just like basketball teams, nongovernmental organizations (NGOs) need to play both games to win consistently. RESULTS has invented a good outside technique and uses it effectively but doesn't have much inside game and therefore loses critical support of important players and makes unneeded mistakes. Other NGOs have a pretty good inside game but need to develop ways to work up a little pressure—or at least the threat of it. Letters, postcards, and the like would help a lot to achieve the ultimate end.

Last night, my team lost by one point in double overtime because the other team got a combination of (outside) three-point baskets and a game winning (inside) lay-up. I think there really is a lesson here.

Do NGOs have both the inside and the outside skills it takes to consistently win in this congressional advocacy game?

Doug Siglin is vice president
for Conservation at American Rivers.

Originally published by InterAction as part of
their Monday Developments Series: 1989, 7 (a).
Reprinted with permission.

Examples of Media Ads and Legislative Alerts

The Results Are In:
America Wants Action on Tobacco Now.

Why Does The Public Want Action?
- 87% are concerned about tobacco use by kids as a public health issue
- 73% agree that a national tobacco policy is important to help parents discourage kids from smoking
- 67% believe that a national tobacco policy is likely to reduce tobacco use by kids

What Does the Public Want?
- 85% want a national minimum age with ID checks
- 83% want to ban vending machines and place all tobacco products behind the counter
- 78% want restrictions on smoking in public places
- 77% want funds for programs to help smokers quit
- 70% want funding for a national prevention/education program
- 60% want full authority for the FDA
- 59% want to increase the price by as much as $1.50 a pack if youth smoking does not decline
- 57% want stiff tobacco industry penalties if youth smoking does not decline

When Do They Want It?
- 72% agree that it is important to establish a national policy now rather than waiting for lawsuits against the industry to conclude
- 71% think it is important that Congress address a national policy in the next six months.

Source: National survey of 1,000 adults, conducted by Market Facts' TeleNation, September 19-25.

It's time to end the nation's tobacco epidemic. Let's get it done.
It's a life saver for America's kids.

American Academy of Family Physicians; American Academy of Pediatrics; American Association for Respiratory Care; American Cancer Society; American College of Chest Physicians; American College of Preventive Medicine; American Heart Association; American Medical Association; American Psychological Association; Campaign for Tobacco-Free Kids; National Association of County and City Health Officials; National Association of Local Boards of Health; Partnership for Prevention; Society for Public Health Education

ENACT (Effective National Action to Control Tobacco)
P.O. Box 65168 • Washington, DC 20035 • (202) 293-1405

The Results Are In:
Michigan Wants Action on Tobacco Now.

Why Do Michigan Residents Want Action?

- 87% are concerned about tobacco use by kids.
- 71% agree that a national tobacco policy is important to help parents discourage their kids from smoking.
- 73% think it is important that Congress address a national tobacco policy in the next six months.

What Do Michigan Residents Want?

- 90% want smoking prohibited in public places.
- 81% want all tobacco products to be placed behind the counter, and other restrictions on youth access to tobacco.
- 72% want to prohibit outdoor advertising and other tobacco marketing aimed at kids.
- 75% want larger and stronger warning labels on cigarette packs.

It's time to end America's tobacco epidemic. We need national legislation. It's a life saver for America's kids.

Tobacco vs. Kids. Where America draws the line.

To learn more, call 1-800-284-KIDS.

This ad sponsored by: American Heart Association, Michigan Affiliate; Michigan State Medical Society; Campaign for Tobacco-Free Kids; The Tri-Cities Tobacco Action Coalition

The National Center for Tobacco-Free Kids • 1707 L Street NW, Suite 800, Washington, DC 20036 • http://www.tobaccofreekids.org

© 1997 National Center for Tobacco-Free Kids

ARKANSAS ORCHESTRAS: IMMEDIATE ACTION NEEDED! SENATOR BUMPERS "UNDECIDED" ABOUT NEA FUNDING

The Senate is currently debating FY98 funding for the NEA. Moments ago, **Sen. Dale Bumpers** (D-AR) stated on the Senate floor that he is undecided about an amendment to increase the amount of NEA funding block-granted to the states. Please contact Sen. Bumpers's office immediately to:

1. Thank him for his statements this morning in support of federal funding for the NEA.

2. Urge him to **oppose** the amendment offered by Sen. Kay Bailey Hutchison (R-TX) to increase the block-grants to the states to 75% of NEA funding. Sen. Bumpers has already indicated that he will oppose an amendment offered by fellow Arkansas Sen. Tim Hutchinson that would block-grant 99% of NEA funds (which we also oppose).

Sen. Bumpers has long been a leader of support for NEA funding in the Senate. It is crucial that he remain firmly in support of the current NEA funding formula (35% of NEA funds go directly to the states). While we support modest increases to 40%, as suggested in S.1020, the Jeffords-Kennedy reauthorization proposal, we oppose further increases that would undermine the NEA's ability to provide federal leadership through direct grants to arts organizations.

To reach Senator Bumpers's office:
CALL: (202) 224-4843
or
FAX: (202) 224-6435

- NEA grants identify projects that act as models for arts organizations nationwide. With a **National** Endowment for the Arts grant, the arts institution is not only awarded money, it receives the **national recognition** it deserves.

- The NEA helps to fund **collaborations that cross state lines**. A number of orchestras provide education outreach programs that are not restricted to their home state alone; state legislators tend not to want state-generated dollars to go out of the state, preferring to emphasize in-state programs. These programs, stimulated by the NEA, serve both the national and local interests.

- Increasing the block-grants to the states is not "more efficient." Until the past two years, the NEA has maintained an administrative level at or below that of most state arts agencies. The recent increase in NEA administrative overhead, deliberately misrepresented by the agency's opponents, was caused by Congress, which mandated deep cuts in funding that necessitated civil service buyouts, internal reorganization, and a whole new grant structure. The NEA has reinvented itself to meet the demands of Congress, and now it is being pilloried by some legislators for "high administrative overhead."

John Sparks, ext. 262, and Heather Watts, ext. 233, Government Affairs   *September 16, 1997*

1156 Fifteenth Street, NW, Suite 800 / Washington, DC 20005-1704
Tel: 202-776-0212 / *Fax:* 202-776-0224 / *E-mail:* league@symphony.org

National Easter Seal Society
Office of Public Affairs

700 Thirteenth Street, N.W., Suite 200
Washington, DC 20005
202 347.3066
202 347.7385 (TDD)
202 737.7914 (fax)

ACTION ALERT

To: **Easter Seal Staff, Volunteers and Families**

From: **Katy Beh Neas, Assistant Vice President,
Government Relations**

Date: **February 2, 1998**

Re: **Congressional child care initiatives**

PRESIDENT CLINTON'S INITIATIVE: Easter Seals staff, volunteers and families responded to the call to action and flooded the White House with phone calls and letters. The President's staff is revising the proposal to include specific provisions to address the child care needs of working families with children with disabilities. WELL DONE!!

NEXT STEPS: Over the coming months, Congress will develop child care legislation to implement the President's proposal. It is vital that Congress hears our message and writes child care legislation that promotes opportunities for all families.

Easter Seals knows that child care providers too often lack the information and supports necessary to effectively meet the child care needs of children with disabilities and their families. Child care providers need access to specific training and to appropriate staff and consultants in order to meet the needs of children with disabilities in a variety of child care settings. These and other systemic supports that are targeted directly at meeting the unique needs of children with disabilities are essential for families with children with disabilities to access child care.

ACTION REQUESTED: Easter Seal staff, volunteers and families are asked to write or telephone their Representatives and Senators. Sample messages and letters are attached. Easter Seals has established a toll-free number that goes directly to the switchboard at the United States Capitol. Simply call 1 (800) 332-2839 and ask to be connected with the office of your Representative or Senator. This telephone line does not connect you to Easter Seals, rather it connects you directly to the Capitol.

Thank you for your assistance with this important activity. Your advocacy will benefit millions of working families with children with disabilities. Please send copies of your letters to the Office of Public Affairs. If you have any questions, please contact Katy Beh Neas at (202) 347-3066, FAX (202) 737-7914, e-mail katy_neas@nessdc.org.

The Easter Seals message:

1. Working families with children with disabilities need access to quality affordable child care just like all other working families.

2. Too often, child care providers lack the information and supports necessary to effectively meet the child care needs of children with disabilities and their families.

3. Congress must develop child care legislation that addresses the fundamental needs of families with children with disabilities.

4. Easter Seals will work with Congress to ensure that all families can benefit from federal child care initiatives.

Sample letter for Easter Seal families

The Honorable_____		The Honorable_____
U.S. House of Representatives	OR	United States Senate
Washington, DC 20515		Washington, DC 20510

Dear Representative	OR	Dear Senator

I am a working parent of a child with a disability. Finding safe child care for my child is very difficult because too many centers and family day care homes won't take in my child.

I understand that Congress will consider legislation to make child care more affordable and accessible, to raise the quality of child care, and to assure the safety of care for millions of children.

Please make sure that all child care legislation addresses the fundamental needs of families with children with disabilities. Easter Seals stands ready to work with you to ensure that all families can benefit from this legislation.

Sincerely,

Sample letter for Easter Seal staff and volunteers

The Honorable_____   The Honorable_____
U.S. House of Representatives   OR   United States Senate
Washington, DC 20515   Washington, DC 20510

Dear Representative   OR   Dear Senator

Easter Seals in ___ serves children and adults with disabilities. Many of the families we serve struggle to find safe, quality child care for their children.

Too often, child care providers lack the information and supports necessary to effectively meet the child care needs of children with disabilities and their families. Child care providers need access to specific training and to appropriate staff and consultants in order to meet the needs of children with disabilities in a variety of child care settings. Easter Seals knows these and other systemic supports that are targeted directly at meeting the unique needs of children with disabilities are essential for families with children with disabilities to access child care.

Please make sure that all child care legislation addresses the fundamental needs of families with children with disabilities. Easter Seals stands ready to work with you to ensure that all families can benefit from this legislation.

Sincerely,

IRS Form 5768

Form **5768** (Rev. December 1996) Department of the Treasury Internal Revenue Service	**Election/Revocation of Election by an Eligible Section 501(c)(3) Organization To Make Expenditures To Influence Legislation** **(Under Section 501(h) of the Internal Revenue Code)**	For IRS Use Only ▶

Name of organization	Employer identification number

Number and street (or P.O. box no., if mail is not delivered to street address)	Room/suite

City, town or post office, and state	ZIP + 4

1 Election—As an eligible organization, we hereby elect to have the provisions of section 501(h) of the Code, relating to expenditures to influence legislation, apply to our tax year ending..and all subsequent tax years until revoked. (Month, day, and year)

Note: *This election must be signed and postmarked within the first taxable year to which it applies.*

2 Revocation—As an eligible organization, we hereby revoke our election to have the provisions of section 501(h) of the Code, relating to expenditures to influence legislation, apply to our tax year ending...
(Month, day, and year)

Note: *This revocation must be signed and postmarked before the first day of the tax year to which it applies.*

Under penalties of perjury, I declare that I am authorized to make this (check applicable box) ▶ ☐ election   ☐ revocation on behalf of the above named organization.

--   ---   -----------------------------
(Signature of officer or trustee)   (Type or print name and title)   (Date)

General Instructions

Section references are to the Internal Revenue Code.

Section 501(c)(3) states that an organization exempt under that section will lose its tax-exempt status and its qualification to receive deductible charitable contributions if a substantial part of its activities are carried on to influence legislation. Section 501(h), however, permits certain eligible 501(c)(3) organizations to elect to make limited expenditures to influence legislation. An organization making the election will, however, be subject to an excise tax under section 4911 if it spends more than the amounts permitted by that section. Also, the organization may lose its exempt status if its lobbying expenditures exceed the permitted amounts by more than 50% over a 4-year period. For any tax year in which an election under section 501(h) is in effect, an electing organization must report the actual and permitted amounts of its lobbying expenditures and grass roots expenditures (as defined in section 4911(c)) on its annual return required under section 6033. See Schedule A (Form 990). Each electing member of an affiliated group must report these amounts for both itself and the affiliated group as a whole.

To make or revoke the election, enter the ending date of the tax year to which the election or revocation applies in item **1** or **2**, as applicable, and sign and date the form in the spaces provided.

Eligible Organizations.—A section 501(c)(3) organization is permitted to make the election if it is not a disqualified organization (see below) and is described in:

1. Section 170(b)(1)(A)(ii) (relating to educational institutions),

2. Section 170(b)(1)(A)(iii) (relating to hospitals and medical research organizations),

3. Section 170(b)(1)(A)(iv) (relating to organizations supporting government schools),

4. Section 170(b)(1)(A)(vi) (relating to organizations publicly supported by charitable contributions),

5. Section 509(a)(2) (relating to organizations publicly supported by admissions, sales, etc.), or

6. Section 509(a)(3) (relating to organizations supporting certain types of public charities other than those section 509(a)(3) organizations that support section 501(c)(4), (5), or (6) organizations).

Disqualified Organizations.—The following types of organizations are not permitted to make the election:

a. Section 170(b)(1)(A)(i) organizations (relating to churches),

b. An integrated auxiliary of a church or of a convention or association of churches, or

c. A member of an affiliated group of organizations if one or more members of such group is described in **a** or **b** of this paragraph.

Affiliated Organizations.—Organizations are members of an affiliated group of organizations only if **(1)** the governing instrument of one such organization requires it to be bound by the decisions of the other organization on legislative issues, or **(2)** the governing board of one such organization includes persons (i) who are specifically designated representatives of another such organization or are members of the governing board, officers, or paid executive staff members of such other organization, and (ii) who, by aggregating their votes, have sufficient voting power to cause or prevent action on legislative issues by the first such organization.

For more details, see section 4911 and section 501(h).

Note: *A private foundation (including a private operating foundation) is not an eligible organization.*

Where To File.—Mail Form 5768 to the Internal Revenue Service Center, Ogden, UT 84201-0027.

Cat. No. 12125M   Form **5768** (Rev. 12-96)

Resource G

Organizations and Information

Organizations

The Advocacy Institute
1730 Rhode Island Avenue, NW, Suite 600
Washington, DC 20036
Tel: (202) 659-8475
Fax: (202) 659-8484
E-mail: info@advocacy.org
Website: www.advocacy.org

Alliance for Justice
2000 P Street, NW, Suite 500
Washington, DC 20036
Tel: (202) 822-6070
Fax: (202) 822-6068
E-mail: advocacy@afj.org
Website: www.afj.org

Charity Lobbying in the Public Interest
2040 S Street, NW
Washington, DC 20009
Tel: (202) 387-5048
Fax: (202) 387-5149
E-mail: Charity.Lobbying@IndependentSector.org
Website: www.IndependentSector.org/clpi

INDEPENDENT SECTOR
1200 Eighteenth Street, NW, Suite 200
Washington, DC 20036
Tel: (202) 467-6100
Fax: (202) 467-6101
E-mail: info@IndependentSector.org
Website: www.IndependentSector.org

OMB Watch
1742 Connecticut Avenue, NW
Washington, DC 20009
Tel: (202) 234-8494
Fax: (202) 234-8584
E-mail: ombwatch@ombwatch.org
Website: www.ombwatch.org/ombwatch

Information

Internal Revenue Service
Tel: 800-829-3676

IRS Tax-Exempt Organizations Website:
www.irs.ustreas.gov/prod/bus_info/eo/
(Form 5768 is available by phone or on the web.)

Mailing address for Form 5768:
IRS Center
Ogden, UT 84201-0027

REFERENCES

American Heart Association. (1984). *Heart and Government: A Guide to Lobbying*. Washington, DC: American Heart Association.

American Lung Association. (1985). *Legislative Network Volunteer Manual*. New York: American Lung Association.

Association of Junior Leagues. (1986). *By the People*. New York: Association of Junior Leagues.

Boisture, B., Sellers, B. 1998. *Power, Politics, and Nonprofits: A Primer on Tax-Exempt Organizations, Campaign Finance, and the Law*. Washington, DC: INDEPENDENT SECTOR.

Burson-Marsteller. (1992). *Attention Congressional Staff Give Selected Communications and Comparative Frequency of Such Communications*. Washington, DC: Burson-Marsteller.

Children's Defense Fund. (1983). *Lobbying and Political Activity for Nonprofits: What You Can (and Can't) Do Under Federal Law*. Washington, DC: Children's Defense Fund.

Duncan, P. and Lawrence, Christine C. *Politics in America, 1998: The 105th Congress*. (1998). Washington, DC: Congressional Quarterly Press.

Gardner, J.W. (1972). *In Common Cause*. New York: Norton.

Grupenhoff, J.T. and Murphy, J. J. (1977). *Nonprofits' Handbook on Lobbying*. Washington, DC: Taft Corporation.

Halperin, S. (1981). *A Guide for the Powerless—and Those Who Don't Know Their Own Power*. Washington, DC: Institution for Educational Leadership.

Hubbard, R. L. (1977). *Lobbying By Public Charities*. Washington, DC: National Center for Voluntary Action/Council for Public Interest Law.

INDEPENDENT SECTOR. (1998). *Playing by the Rules: Handbook on Voter Participation and Education Work for 501(c)(3) Organizations*. Washington, DC: INDEPENDENT SECTOR.

INDEPENDENT SECTOR. n.d. *Lobby? You?* Washington, DC: INDEPENDENT SECTOR.

Internal Revenue Service. (1977). *Revenue Ruling E:0:1-1*. Washington, DC: Internal Revenue Service.

Lustberg, A. (1982). *Testifying with Impact*. Washington, DC: U.S. Chamber of Commerce.

National Mental Health Association. 1989. *A Layman's Guide to Lobbying Without Losing Your Tax-Exempt Status.* Alexandria, VA: National Mental Health Association.

National Society for Children and Adults with Autism. (1985). *NSAC Action.* Washington, DC: National Society for Children and Adults with Autism.

O'Connell, B. (1994). *The Board Member's Book.* New York: Foundation Center.

O'Connell, B. (1994). *People Power: Service, Advocacy, Empowerment.* New York: Foundation Center.

O'Connell, B. (1981). *Effective Leadership in Voluntary Organizations.* New York: Walker & Co.

Ornstein, N.J., and Elder, S. (1978). *Interests Groups, Lobbying and Policy Making.* Washington, DC: Congressional Quarterly Press.

Regan v. *Taxation With Representation of Washington.* (1983). 461 U.S. 540, 545 n. 6.

Rubin, B. (1997). *A Citizen's Guide to Politics in America: How the System Works and How to Work the System.* New York: M.E. Sharpe, Inc.

Talisman, M.E. (1977). *The Legislative Process.* Washington, DC: Council of Jewish Federation.

Webster, G. D., and Krebs, F. J. (1985). *Association and Lobbying Regulation.* Washington, DC: U.S. Chamber of Commerce.

Index

voter education, 66–68, 118
    candidates' statements and, 67
    electioneering and, 66
    issue briefings for candidates'
        statements, 68
    public forums and, 68
    questionnaires and, 67
    testimony on party platforms and, 68
    voting records and, 67
voting records, 1976 lobby law and, 67

W

websites, 19–20
    for legislative alerts, 18
    organizations and information, 133
White House Comment Line, 31

Y

Yahoo, 19
YMCA of the USA, 90–91

Z

zip code matching, 21